SNAKE'S *daughter*

SINGULAR LIVES

The Iowa Series in

North American Autobiography

Albert E. Stone, Series Editor

SNAKE'S *daughter*

THE ROADS IN AND OUT OF WAR

Gail Hosking Gilberg

UNIVERSITY OF IOWA PRESS Ψ IOWA CITY

University of Iowa Press, Iowa City 52242

Copyright © 1997 by the University of Iowa Press

Printed in the United States of America

Design by Richard Hendel

http://www.uiowa.edu/~uipress

Printed on acid-free paper

Library of Congress Cataloging-in-Publication Data

Gilberg, Gail Hosking, 1950–

Snake's daughter: the roads in and out of war / Gail Hosking Gilberg.

p.   cm.–(Singular lives)

Includes bibliographical references.

ISBN 0-87745-585-6, ISBN 0-87745-586-4 (pbk.)

1. Hosking, Charles, 1924–1967. 2. United States. Army–
Biography. 3. Vietnamese Conflict. 1961–1975. I. Title.
II. Series.

U53.H67G55   1997

355'.0092–dc21

[b]   96-49229

01 00 99 98 97 C 5 4 3 2 1
01 00 99 98 97 P 5 4 3 2 1

To the memory of my parents,

CHARLES ERNEST HOSKING, JR.,

and

GLORIA WALTERS.

To my sons,

DAVID *and* BENJAMIN,

who made the writing of

this book very important.

CONTENTS

War is like a giant pack rat.

It takes something from you, and it

leaves something in its stead.

—Audie Murphy, 1955

The earth will recover.

The daughter will revive in the spring;

you can see in your mind's eye, radiant,

death's kingdom behind her,

a blood-red poppy in her hair.

—Lynne Hanley,

"Planting Tulips," in

Writing War: Fiction, Gender

and Memory

Foreword by *Albert E. Stone*

G ail Hosking Gilberg's *Snake's Daughter: The Roads in and out of War* is, quite simply, an arresting and anguished narrative. It aptly illustrates the rewards and the costs of confronting and recovering the personal past. This is an account of life and death – life in the Regular Army from the enlisted man's point of view, the death in Vietnam of one very human and exemplary warrior, the father of the autobiographer. Women looking at war (and at Vietnam in particular, which some squeamish Americans persist in calling the "Vietnam Conflict") is an age-old story now made freshly pertinent, for our country shows few signs of living up to ex–President Bush's confident declaration that Desert Storm finally put the Vietnam syndrome to rest. Gilberg is surely correct to point out contrary evidence: the continuing dearth of accurate governmental information (e.g., on MIAs) and the spate of personal stories (novels, nonfiction accounts, autobiographies, films) that keep the pain and politics of Vietnam alive in many imaginations. One such disturbing personal narrative is Peg Mullen's *Unfriendly Fire: A Mother's Memoir* (Iowa, 1995). The overlaps and contrasts between these two volumes in the Singular Lives series are numerous and revealing.

For one thing, the mother's and the daughter's stories turn upon a single center – the day of the deaths in Vietnam of two sergeants. Both accounts, too, move forward from fateful dates (March 21, 1967, for "Snake" Hosking, February 18, 1970, for Michael Mullen) to very recent acts of writing each woman's autobiography. Both writers are, moreover, still wracked with anger. Perhaps because Gilberg is younger – she was only seventeen when her father died – her story dwells heavily on family life before that day. Not motivated like Mullen to political protest, Gilberg struggles inwardly to make sense of her life and identity. "I've drawn a line between myself and the rest of the country. I know that's not true. Nothing, not one single thing in life, is that simple. Then what does a daughter of a dead warrior do all these years later? . . . How does she find peace, and I don't mean just the absence of war?"

Search for final peace starts with a protracted encounter with finding words. It also entails dealing with photographic images of Gilberg's three pasts — growing up as an army brat, facing the young soldier at the door who brings word of her father's death near the Song Be River, and the decades of living, often in suppressed suffering, with that loss. Thus a signal feature of this narrative is the interplay of written word and snapshots rescued from family albums and her father's effects. For years the posthumous Medal of Honor recipient tried to save and say with a camera what he couldn't put into words. His was a seesaw existence that moved between stern discipline and alcoholism, caution and courage, constant moving and impatient waiting in peace and war, promotion and demotion, allegiance to comrades that undercut devotion to an often-distant family of loving but insecure dependents. Like father, like daughter. "The camera captured what my body carries around to this day," she remarks of her girlish images in those albums. Yet she has learned a higher allegiance to words. "The warrior's daughter grows up to write what it means to be just that. She writes to find her own identity, to retaliate against the dismembering of her father, to offset the forgetting. She writes to recreate life, to remove one of those body bags from the mass. She knows that only a writer can answer some questions and that she will find her father on the pages she writes."

Discovery, she finds, revolves around fleeting but vital details, not a broad map. One is the wedding ring missing from her father's finger as he stands in a snapshot beside a comrade (who clearly wears *his* ring) in the jungle. In this tiny punctum (Roland Barthes's term, which she uses to describe a key entry point inside the surface of a photograph) Gilberg symbolizes the story of her parents' ill-fated marriage. It also underlines her own allegiance to both, as she recovers in this absent ring the reality of a love slowly eroded by the years-long pressures of an army dependent's lonely life of waiting. Over and over, she dramatizes the self-sacrificing death of her father, who tackled a VC prisoner holding a grenade to save his comrades' lives at the price of his own. This, in stark contrast with the lonely death of her divorced and then alcoholic mother, who simply died leaning over the sink in a shabby stateside kitchen. "If I could only capture the room's smells, you might better know the places that lie under the map," she writes of the lost pasts of parents and daughters. "Or the smell of my mother's life tumbling into small crevices as she struggled each time to climb out. . . . I write to understand why hunger washes over me in the loneliness of dusk."

Gail Gilberg has emerged, scathed but intact, from this battle with time and death. The sensitivity and vigor of her re-creation attest to an achieved self who has looked beneath the surfaces of memories, photographs, and other memorabilia, the behavior of families and friends, and her country's history of evasion and embrace of Vietnam. Because the public embrace has served political and military ends that she, like Peg Mullen, cannot endorse, she treats with marked irony a central public ceremony. This took place on one of her visits to Washington. She and her family (but not her mother, uninvited by the Pentagon because divorced just before the hero's death) were invited to the White House, where President Nixon presented them the Congressional Medal of Honor. Utterly without irony is her account of a second Washington visit. With her husband and sons, she stood before the Vietnam Memorial Wall. Like thousands of other Americans, her tear-streaked cheeks bore witness to a personal and national past that cannot be expunged. Equally devoid of ironic distance is the daughter's description of her father's burial in the family cemetery in Paramus, New Jersey. "I recall Special Forces soldiers in full dress uniform standing in the background as they gave a gun salute. I remember the sound of their rifles being slapped by white gloved hands. I remember the stillness of the air. The American flag that draped the coffin was folded into a triangle and handed to my then six-year-old brother." At such moments, the army brat proudly embraces her family's past, whose pain and losses in several wars are in part redeemed by patriotism and the loyalty of soldiers to one another.

Gilberg, born and raised a nondenominational Protestant but now a convert to Judaism, knows that sacrifice, death, loyalty, and love of country may coexist, as they did in the experience of Charles "Snake" Hosking. If in the process wife and children were also sacrificed, that, too, was part of a warrior's fate. "Only in writing can heroism and abandonment live daily side by side," Finvola Drury writes. In truth, writing an autobiography has meant daily immersion in death and other questions it raises.

"Already six of my father's soldier friends haved died during the time it has taken me to write this book." *Snake's Daughter* becomes, therefore, an extended meditation on death in the America of the Vietnam era. "Then why did he finally get killed, I ask my uncle? Did he know that he was choosing death when he jumped on the back of the Vietcong prisoner running with a grenade toward the other soldiers?"

Answers to such anguished questions have come slowly. They arrived often at dusk or night in the painfully solitary act of setting down words on a page. One of the most poignant weavings-together of these remembrances comes near the middle of this narrative.

I often think of the many opposites of my father: generous but selfish, qualified but disabled, fearless but fearful. I imagine he spent his life wrestling with these opposites. I know now without a doubt, as only those who struggle a long time with a question can come to know, that my father knew what he was doing when he wrapped his arms around the prisoner. I believe he wanted not only to save the Vietnamese and American soldiers in the path of the grenade, but he wanted more than anything to reclaim the self he knew he was losing through divorce and the changes in America. The world he had known was coming apart at the seams.

Although the autobiographer has reached these beliefs only slowly and in separation, the reach of her education embraces many friends and family members. Among these remembered are her two younger sisters. In girlhood the three often fought fiercely for their father's intermittent attention and their mother's caresses. "Three separate, three different women have emerged from those times and have sought each other out as if no one else would ever do. Our contact, our separate memories we bring to the visits help cradle the loss that still permeates our lives. . . . They, who wore the same dresses I once wore, remember the sound of my father's stern voice, my mother's cry, the softness of her young skin. They know what it is that will bring me to tears, how my aloofness doesn't mean I don't care. I recognize when their humor is hiding great pain, and I know how to keep their secrets."

Here, as elsewhere, emotional truth is conveyed through tiny details. After years of suppression, memories now overcome forgetting in such domestic images as the look of front stoops on army dependents' apartments, the sounds of parents arguing in the night, a mother's red stretch belt, the flavor of her banana pudding. Only stories can exhibit the truths behind these "divine details," a phrase of Vladimir Nabokov that Gilberg is understandably fond of. Back then, the reserved eldest sister "learned to stuff fragments deep into my gut." Now, "my story gets burdened with the visual and the smells I pack into capsules of time and place." Just as her dead father once used his camera to try to put a frame around the lives of his family, so now the daughter reaches for images and facts to compose a satisfactory explanation. The process often brought her close to nervous collapse. Once, she called a government archivist in search of documents on the Special Forces, the famous Green Berets her father served with in Vietnam. "I wanted contact with my father, wanted to see what it was he saw." But such records, she learned, are nonexistent: "tons of records were shredded and what remained, if anything, was sent up to the National Archives in Washington, D.C. 'I guess you could call it "forced amnesia,"' he said."

In a reflection triggered by this official's response, Gail Gilberg reaches the emotional and moral plateau on which Peg Mullen so often dwells in *Unfriendly Fire.*

I thought if I could memorize its sound I could allow myself to believe that what my father had fought for had been shredded, as if in doing so this country could move on to the next "conflict," move on before it looked too closely or asked too many questions of its higher ups. . . . But the phone call reminded me that we are a nation who is forgetting. We are no different now than in the Civil War when Walt Whitman wrote that the real war would never get into the books. . . . I would remember what this country wants to forget. Making this book is a counterattack to the shredding. I am back in the field putting together my father's mutilated body, limb by limb, remembering what was once dismembered. I am removing the masks of secrecy, stoicism, and denial I learned as an army brat. I am offsetting this forced amnesia.

In passionate meditations like these the author of *Snake's Daughter* succeeds, I believe, in lifting the weight of silent anguish long afflicting her. In the process, this private self exposes public myths and realities about the Vietnam era that might be displayed only through the eyes of an army brat who was an enlisted man's daughter. Her exploration of the multiple meanings of one soldier's death recalls, even as it recasts and maybe even challenges, some famous lines of an American poet. In "For the Union Dead" Robert Lowell writes about war, heroism, and death. His poem was republished in 1964, at the same time Sergeant Snake Hosking was serving the first of three tours of duty in Vietnam. Lowell celebrates much earlier Civil War deaths, those of Colonel Robert Shaw and the black troops he led into battle at Fort Wagner, South Carolina. Most were slaughtered there, including the young white officer. They are depicted in Augustus St. Gauden's bronze memorial in Boston. Lowell writes that Shaw "is out of bounds now. He rejoices in man's lovely, peculiar power to choose life and die − / When he leads his black soldiers to death he cannot bend his back."

Snake Hosking and Robert Shaw are as different in their lives and deaths as in some respects they are similar. What marks *Snake's Daughter* as a significant document of our era is that a private woman in early middle age has written a double story that sounds like self-sacrifice but is really one of self-reclamation. Her narrative is, therefore, much closer in spirit to Walt Whitman's *Specimen Days* than to Lowell's "For the Union Dead." She has liberated in her own and her father's words, through his and others' photographs, voices from the usually hidden recordings of a recent war. Through a daughter's eyes and ears we can recognize vicariously one whose name, rank, and date of death are recorded also on that smooth sloping wall in Washington.

Acknowledgments

his book could never have been written in isolation. It took the resources of many who believed in the importance of my writing about my father. So many people gave of their time and encouragement.

I want to acknowledge the soldiers who answered my plea for anecdotes and memories about my father. They called and wrote from all over the United States and led me story by story back to him. Sometimes it was just a paragraph, and other times they wrote pages of memories and sent books they thought would help me understand my father, photographs, a Mike Force scarf, pictures of their families, and Christmas cards. They were my connection back to the military. I would like to thank Al Arellano, Manfield Baier, Mark Berent, Fred Boggs, Elmo Clark, Jim Clark, Isaac Camacho, Thomas E. Corbett, Fred Davis (deceased), Jimmy Dean at the *Drop*, Ed Doggett, David Charles Dolby, Jim Donahue, Charlie Doyle, Jim Edgell, Charles Fergusen, Sully de Fontaine, Alexander Fontes, Bill Fuller, Hugh Gordon, Bo Gritz, Ervin (Dutch) Harpole, McBert Higgenbotham (deceased), Howard Hill, Frank Iacabelli, Jan Janasac, Jim Keen, William A. (Buck) Kindoll (deceased), John Kingerter, Dennis Lamb, Joe Lopez, Joe Mancusco, Roy Matthews, Mike McCarthy, Harry McGlouglin (deceased), Chuck McNulty, Jim Monaghan, Bill Nolte (deceased), Col. Charles Norton (retired), Michael O'Connor, Lester Parrish (deceased), Charles Petty, Bill Ramsdell, John Roy, Newman Ruff, Peter Sheerin, Steve Sherman, Les Silvernail, Robert Simmons, Robert Skyles, Marion Spicer, G. E. Stanford, Shelby Stanton, Earl Tanner, and William Yarborough. A special thanks to Col. Charles Norton for doing research for me at the National Archives.

I wish also to acknowledge the Thirteenth Airborne Division Association, Thomas Stiles, Thomas Connolly, Tom Dater, Roxanne Merritt at the Fort Bragg JFK Musuem, Norman Stegan, the *Static Line*, the *Drop*, the Special Forces Association, Richard Reeves, and the Honorable Louise Slaughter.

I wish to acknowledge the *South Dakota Review*, in which "Late Night Photographs" and "Underneath the Map: Rooms of

War and Perpetual Dusk" first appeared in altered form, and the *Chattahoochee Review*, in which *"Mētis"* first appeared.

Thanks to John Lovenheim for his computer expertise and his willingness to help me at a moment's notice.

Many thanks are due Richard Margolis, whose talent as a photographer taught me much about viewing photographs and the pace of art.

Thanks to Dr. Colin Murray Turbayne, professor emeritus of philosophy at the University of Rochester, for kindly allowing me to use his quiet and uninhabited house so that I could finish this book without interruption.

I would like to thank my sisters, Elizabeth Evans and Janice Brazil, for lending me their photograph albums, giving me copies of letters and family records, and cheering me on throughout this project. They were both a steady ear and a wealth of memories. Thanks also to my brother-in-law Roy J. Evans, who kept finding family records in his files and sending them to me.

My father's brother, Robert Hosking, patiently filled in the many blanks of my father's time line, made phone calls for me, and was always there when I called him with yet another question. His support and love have been with me for a very long time, and I could never have come to write this book without him.

Many thanks as well to my grandmother Luella Hosking, whose life of one hundred years has seen many things and whose clear memories helped pave my way.

Thanks to my teachers along the way: Mary Jo Iuppa, Judith Kitchen, Bob Shacochis, and Susan Cheever. They gave just the right amount of critical analysis and always the right amount of encouragement. Their talents and support helped me through the difficulty of the writing process.

My friend, teacher, and writing mentor, Finvola Drury, was an essential voice and ear throughout the entire writing of this book. Our faithful correspondence opened up my view of the subject of my father. She offered wise guidance, book and movie titles, concepts to think about, and a skillful judgment of my prose. She was tireless in her patience, devotion, and affection and championed this book when it scarcely existed. Her civilian voice helped steer me through many difficult moments and convinced me that "writing is the bridge from the magical thinking of childhood to the reconstruction of the lost reality." She led me across that bridge and into the place of writing, where I have found my father. My heartfelt and everlasting gratitude goes out to her.

Finally, I thank my family for their patience with me for the years it took to write this book. My husband, Bruce, supported me in all the ways that allowed me to sit for hours at the computer, leave for writing classes, and spend months at a time preoccupied with my father's life. His belief in me and his love have sustained me now for more than a quarter of a century. I am eternally blessed.

Introduction

It's difficult to know where to begin the story of my father's life. Should I start with the man whose name is carved on panel 17E, line 5, of the Vietnam Memorial Wall and work backward, or should I begin with his running away from home at age sixteen to join the Canadian army and go forward from there? Perhaps it doesn't matter. Either way I end up looking at his death — a death that either has been or will be.

Survivors who knew him tell me my father had an invincible quality about him. He survived the Second World War in the 509th Paratrooper Infantry Battalion: only forty-seven out of its six hundred men were left on their feet after the Battle of the Bulge. While stationed in Europe with the Special Forces in the 1950s, he was hand-picked for secret missions into Africa. It was said he trained hard, kept the morale of the others up, and had a "resourceful knowledge of foreign weapons." During the Vietnam War, when he went back for the third time to rejoin the "Mike Force," others volunteered when they heard "the Snake" had returned. He was so legendary with the Chinese Nung and Cambodian soldiers after his first tour of duty there that when he came back to Vietnam, several came out of retirement to fight with him.

My father was a man of many opposites. His high IQ gave him opportunities to become an officer, but he enjoyed being "at the bottom with the best," as he repeatedly said. He was a private person and yet a team player. He joined a subculture that stressed order and precision, and within it he found his personal way of doing things — he was an "outlaw," as a fellow soldier described him. My father was not a religious person, and yet he spent his R&R free time doing what was unusual for American soldiers in Vietnam to do — visiting Buddhist monks. When I was a child, he made my sisters and me go to Sunday school every Sunday; we weren't allowed to play outside the rest of the day if we didn't. But he never went to church himself. I would come home and find him washing the car — something I was taught in Sunday school one wasn't supposed to do on the Sabbath.

He was intensely patriotic but felt most at home on foreign soil and speaking other languages — among them, Vietnamese, an accomplishment for any Westerner. Friends describe my father as a sensitive man, capable of deep feelings, yet he spent his whole adult life in a society that taught him to compartmentalize his feelings. He loved his family, but at important moments he was always someplace else.

As I look back, I know I lived constantly with my father's greatest paradox. By nature his work was contradictory, full of puzzles. He was a professional soldier, a job he got paid for and which paid the family bills. Like other fathers, he went to work Monday through Friday from nine to five, and most of the time nothing happened. But the false proposition of his seemingly secure work was that sometimes, even on routine training exercises, some things did happen. Once a bazooka weapon exploded by accident at Fort Campbell and killed all the men in front of my father, but not him. Such was the unspoken side of his life. He lived with death, which he buried with duty, determination, and drink. This part he never shared.

Sometimes in the middle of the night, my father would silently pack his gear and leave. In the morning he wouldn't be home. The army called it "maneuvers," as if it were only a game. But it was really a rehearsal for conflict. When called on alert, my father wouldn't know if it was a real war or not, or even where his parachute might land. He knew only that he was to have his gear prepared and be ready to follow orders.

Our household changed when he left. His need for order went with him, creating a more relaxed mood at home. At the same time, his leaving made us feel left without direction, and we struggled to carry on without him. We never knew where he was or how long he'd be gone. Even in the quiet of home there was a lingering sense of our own readiness, as if we too were waiting for a disaster, some military crisis that would inevitably change our lives at a moment's notice. The unspoken potential for loss hung in the air.

Whole chunks of our father's life were off-limits to us. When he returned, we never heard about where he went or what he saw. I don't recall anyone ever saying out loud that we weren't to ask questions, but we children knew that anyway. As I grew up, the gap between my father and me widened, and I knew less and less about him. The army asked a great deal of its dependents, without ever verbalizing it. We were to support my father's comings and goings, not distract him in any way, and go along with any regulations or change in orders. We were the silent, unpaid staff in the background, growing accustomed to the military's way of life with every year my father remained a soldier. We knew no other life. Orders were orders.

In our time together, my father stressed manners and discipline with us. To him it was important how we sat at the table, how we sipped our soup, how we greeted those who spoke to us. He insisted I follow through on projects I began, like the scrapbook of my life he helped me start. I remember his carefully gluing in an aerial view of our base in Germany with an arrow pointing to our apartment, building 106, C-2. Under it he placed my third-grade class photograph into the four photograph corners and showed me where to glue a birthday card from my grandmother across the ocean in New Jersey.

In doing so, I see now how he instilled a structure and a self-reliance within me that was the gift he left behind. It was a form to live with and provided in the years since his death a link to all other worlds I've entered and a method of working with the materials of my life. He wanted for my sisters, brother, and me what he wanted for himself: not to be "just an ordinary GI on the streets," as he repeatedly counseled other soldiers and his family. He wanted us to have the discipline and manners that could carry us in and out of anywhere we wanted to go.

My father taught me to ski and encouraged me when I didn't think I could learn. He read fairy tales out loud from the orange Childcraft books he bought from a traveling salesman. He insisted I make good grades in school and often helped me with my homework. I don't remember what we talked about at the table as I did my math problems and he shined his black army boots, waxing them in small strokes with a stained rag until they shone, or took apart his guns piece by piece and put them back together in blind memory. In those days, I thought all fathers did this, as I thought all fathers were born with tattoos on their arms.

My father loved to travel, and he took us on many trips. In the summer of my eleventh year, we camped along the beach in Barcelona, Spain. He took us to a bullfight on a hot afternoon, and while he described everything that was happening — jumping from his seat with cries of victory when the matador was successful — my sisters and I were more interested in buying cold drinks. We fanned ourselves with our paper fans, and he teased us about covering our eyes. That night, my mother found my father in a bar with my youngest sister, Betty Ann, on his lap. He was drinking and laughing with a group of local Spaniards. Other summers we picnicked along a Bavarian lake called the Tegernsee, hiked in the German Alps, or visited King Ludwig's castles. In France, he insisted we visit cemeteries of Second World War soldiers. The white crosses, interrupted by a Star of David now and then, lined up across the field at an angle more perfect than I have ever seen since.

When I was twelve — still singing songs with my Girl Scout troop about "making new friends, but keeping the old, one is silver and the other gold" — my parents thought of separating. On a cold, winter day we children and my mother boarded the USNS *General William O. Darby* at the port of Bremerhaven, Germany, and headed for the United States. A cold breeze blew that day, creating white-capped waves that surrounded the ship even before it left the harbor. My mother stood on deck with her black jacket trimmed with white fur around the hood. We left my father as the ship blew its loud horn. I remember carrying my pet white mouse, Nancy, in a covered basket, my rock collection in a trunk, and my heart in a steel box. We waved good-bye to my soldier-father, who remained on shore, and it is only today as I write this that I wonder how he let us all go in one swoop. It was 1963, one of the most painful years of my life, branded by the awareness of a family's unraveling.

Within six months, my parents changed their minds about their separation, and they pulled up together at my grandmother's house in a brand new white Ford Falcon station wagon. They came to pick up my sisters and me, and we drove to North Carolina. Even as we settled into new schools, his orders came for Vietnam. He never lived with us for more than a few months at a time after that, and it never seemed the same with my parents again. It was as if I was already witnessing their love fading like the sun disappearing below the horizon. Though he would come home after a tour of duty, he never seemed to find his bearings.

While many fathers went to Vietnam once, my father kept going back until he died there.

Once on one of his return trips home, he sat on the floor of our apartment wearing black Vietnamese pajamalike clothes, eating rice with chopsticks. While we ate meat loaf and mashed potatoes at the table, we listened to him speak about the men he left behind. I see now that the magical country of Vietnam had taken over his life, just like the war and the men at his side who became the reasons for fighting the war. Vietnam had a curious hold on my father I couldn't begin to understand then.

On another visit home, he went with me to a high school football game dressed in his full military dress uniform. I had spent my life seeing him in uniform, and I knew he took it seriously. His pants were tucked into his polished black boots and all his insignia were aligned in their proper places. But that night as he stood on the bleachers dressed differently from anyone else, surrounded by civilians, I began to feel uncomfortable. It confused me. Had I known the right words then, I would have asked what it was all about: the war, the uniform, his always going away. I don't remember one person in that small midwestern town ever once speaking about the war. And if they did, I don't ever remember listening. The loneliness of living within two worlds that never touched often brought me to tears, alone in my bedroom. I would lie on my bed and cry for hours curled up like a baby, never once knowing at the time what the tears were about.

In the weeks before my seventeenth birthday, my father sent me a string of Mikimoto pearls he had bought in either Saigon or Hong Kong. It arrived inside a green velvet box lined with white satin. On the outside yellow cardboard box he wrote with a red pen that he hoped I received the pearls in time for the prom and that he could hardly believe I was seventeen years old. At first I felt they must have been for my mother because I understood myself to be too young for pearls. I imagine, in his sense of formality, he saw these perfectly shaped white pearls as something every young woman should have.

On the first day of spring that same year, only a week after my seventeenth birthday, my father was killed at the age of forty-two. After crossing the Song Be River under sniper fire on a single span of a blown-up bridge lying about a foot under the surface of the water, my father captured a sniper and prepared to link up with his command group. Realizing the prisoner would need his arms to get across the river, my father began to untie the rope. The prisoner suddenly grabbed a hand grenade from my father's belt and began running toward the company command group, which consisted of two American and two Vietnamese soldiers. Realizing the prisoner intended to kill the men, my father leaped on the prisoner's back and grasped him in a bear hug, forcing the grenade against the prisoner's chest. With my father's background of precision and experience, he had to have known that what he did in that instance would surely mean his own death. My father wrestled the prisoner to the ground and covered his body until the grenade detonated. The blast killed both the prisoner and my father instantly.

Twenty-six years later, Jim Monaghan, a fellow Mike Force soldier, calls to tell me he identified my father's body by the tattoos on his arms, remembering to this day the blue-green parachute wings and the motto underneath: "Infantry, Queen of Battle." He wishes he could find and give me the address of Capt. Angelo Canale, who was one of the men my father saved and who went on to retire as a general.

Early in the war, yellow cabs delivered the death notices. People speak now of having lived in fear of seeing a yellow cab in their neighborhood, of having heart attacks when a yellow cab pulled into their driveway. By the time my father was killed, the army sent soldiers as messengers — young soldiers whose duty it was to knock on the doors of strangers and speak the terrifyingly intimate words of death. Our messenger stood in his pressed uniform and polished black boots in the cold March air, telling us words he had memorized. My father, he said, had been killed in the line of duty near the Song Be River. The other details became a blur to me, and I only heard him ask where the army should send the body. After he left, my sisters and my mother and I sat in our apartment with the shades pulled down. My sisters cried, and my mother sat quietly in shock. My six-year-old brother, wearing the Special Forces jungle hat my father had sent him, looked at us in confusion, then continued to play with his toys. I couldn't cry then. I was afraid the whole world might cave in if I did. I remember to this day how I got dressed and left for a date with my boyfriend. From that moment, I erected walls around my heart.

Two years later, in the spring of 1969, when my sisters, brother, and I were living with my Uncle Bob and Aunt Val in New Jersey, we were invited to the White House to receive my father's Congressional Medal of Honor, posthumously awarded. It was like anyone can imagine: a basket of fruit in our fancy hotel room, dinners out with military staff, a trip around Washington, D.C., a private tour of the White House, and then the formal presentation by President Nixon and Melvin Laird, secretary of defense. The ceremony was well planned, and we were all told where to stand and what to do. I remember looking down at the president's shiny black shoes, my face mirrored in them, and feeling as if I were watching a movie of someone else's life. When he bent over to shake the small hand of my eight-year-old brother, I noticed the black waves of the president's hair and thought for a second I saw a private tenderness in the eyes of the men surrounding him. Afterward, he invited my grandmother to see the Rose Garden. They were gone about half an hour, which seemed to make the presidential aides quite nervous, as it was an unplanned gesture. The next day I flew back to college in upstate New York and blended into the crowd with my lips held shut.

Years of rationalizing about my father's death followed; I felt like my path was gone, dropped off the edge. I told a friend his death had been "all for the best," as if I really believed it. I said public opinion about the military was turning negative and that my father wouldn't be happy in uniform or in civilian life. Out of the corner of my eye, I noticed my friend with a curious, confused look on his face, but he didn't say anything. Even so, I tried to show that I could bear my father's death. After all, hadn't my life with the military taught me to "carry on"? Wasn't I the "real trooper" my father had taught me to be?

But as the years went on, a terrible vague sadness would erupt at unexpected moments. At a stop sign once while in my car, I turned to see a Memorial Day army exhibition taking place in the park. An older soldier in the distance directed a helicopter where to land. As a country-western tune – the kind of music I had heard in every snack bar on every base I had ever lived – played on my radio, I burst into tears. The naive phrase "for the best" flashed across my mind, and I felt a sudden loneliness. I wondered how it would be to have a father.

Another time, when I was carrying my second child, I stood alongside my curly-haired husband and three-year-old blond son before the Vietnam Memorial Wall, looking at my pregnant reflection in the shiny black granite. My husband, Bruce, wasn't sure what to say as he held my hand and tried to keep an eye on our son as well. I had come for the first time, wanting to show them my father's name and to see why it was that so many people talked about this wall. A mother had left a letter, now framed, to her son and had placed his teddy bear next to it. I thought my heart would break as I fell to my knees. I felt, for the first time, the immensity of this war and all those lives that never returned home. "I'd give anything to have you shell just one more pecan for me on grandma's porch," a woman named Anne wrote on a note left for her cousin Eddie Lynn Lancaster, who died the same year my father did. I left this sacred ground only to return again, each time my view of the war reaching out farther and farther.

At the wall I saw that I was a mixture of the Asian and American way. I had identified with the Asian way of making my way around something wrong rather than confronting it. And yet there I was facing this wall head on, confronting it in my quiet but American way. In the years to come, I was to learn more of this Asian concept of standing still through pain instead of moving away from it, and I was to become more bold in my American acknowledgment of this wall that had been built to heal our Vietnam War wounds.

Going through my desk drawers years after seeing the wall, I found a photograph of my father eating with chopsticks in Vietnam. He was the only American in the picture. Everything about him was familiar: his olive-drab uniform, his dog tags peering out from under his collar, and his blond hair combed back from his receding hairline. The place, with sandbags piled up behind him and Vietnamese soldiers standing next to him, suddenly seemed odd to me. I realized how little I knew about my father, that even all the photographs I *did* have of him still couldn't tell his story.

Around the time I found the photograph, I had quit my teaching job with no idea why I wanted to get rid of it. When my children went back to school in the fall, I took a drawing class — a lesson, I was to learn later, in how to see. Signing up for the class was one of those seemingly spur-of-the-moment decisions. Odd, I thought, since I wasn't an artist and I had no interest in drawing. Just as I felt strongly compelled to sign up for the drawing class, I signed up for an autobiography and memoir workshop — still with no notion of how the discipline of observation and writing would carry me through a project I hadn't even begun.

At this juncture I began experiencing a burden and a desire I had carried around since my teenage years without ever being aware of them. I needed suddenly to know my father, to talk about war, to understand the life I had come from and how it had affected who I was. I wanted, I now see, what Richard Powers writes about in his novel of the First World War, *Three Farmers on Their Way to a Dance:* a catharsis of my memory and a recognition of my history.

As I studied the first photograph of my father that I found, I realized that my father was my age. Suddenly I had caught up to him. The distance between us shifted, and I was no longer the child. I looked at him as if looking at myself, wanting to know more. His age exposed his humanness, and I felt ready to explore that. I searched for other photographs and found several albums and boxes of slides: pictures of my father, his friends, the places he saw, and his family. They were neither unique nor sensational but had been collected by my father over time as if he knew early on he'd need to document his life for the next generation. He wasn't an artist, nor did he propose to be a photographer, but he did fiddle with film and camera when others might not have. I had known about the photographs but had never before given them more than a quick look. He organized the pictures by month and year — all neatly labeled by a man constantly on the move. Suddenly I wondered why? Why did he make this effort? Did he know I wouldn't have him around when I grew older? Did he want me to remember him and understand him, even though he could no longer speak? Did he know that his images would someday spark my own lost words?

My writing mentor and friend, Finvola Drury, suggested that the photograph collection was a gift. That perhaps my father had come back into my life now as a guide, and that through the photographs he would lead me to address all the questions and feelings I had allowed to surface. He had come and gone as he had done all my childhood, and now he was back. In this way, she said, he had stayed around longer than most fathers. The photographs were all I had left of him, and I felt he wanted me to look at them carefully. It occurs to me now that that same old sense of my father's formal precision and discipline was helping me recreate my life. At times, as I spoke to his buddies on the phone, listened to Finvola's compelling interest and insightful connections, or sat at my desk late at night, pen in hand and tears in my eyes, I felt that we were all working together. I felt beckoned on this journey to find my father.

At first, entering many of his photographs was like getting through a guarded gate. Behind the entrance sat the world a daughter can't know intimately — men and the military. I asked questions for the first time about a society in which I had learned never to ask questions. In searching the photographs I listened to their silence, waiting for details to rise on their own. I stared, sometimes through a magnifying glass, looking at moments that stopped when his camera clicked.

Over time, as the details of the photographs enlarged, I began seeing life in the flat images. I could swear, after a reverent look, that I saw a knee move or a puff of smoke actually come out of someone's cigarette. I felt his sun's heat, and I heard a helicopter buzzing in the distant sky. A leaf ruffled with the breeze, and I walked into the photographs. The photographs' places seized me, and I could no longer remember not being there.

What I found even more difficult in my search was something I had not been aware of before, something the photographs could not show. I realized I would have to struggle to move among and overcome the clichés of the Vietnam era — both those of the military and those opposed to the war. The loss of my father was an obvious pain, but not so the other wounds made by the war. Many in this country, peers and soldiers included, wanted to draw a line between those who fought and those who opposed. Some wanted to believe that men who went to Vietnam were fools or bloodthirsty types, and that nothing good ever happens in war. They believed that the strong were absolutely strong and the weak were absolutely weak. What was and remains is the gray area in between — the most difficult to look at. Just as with my father's photograph collection, no part can stand for the whole, no whole can stand for its parts. Melville said about his Civil War *Battle-Pieces* that the war was "an upheaval affecting the basis of things"— more suffered than understood.

During the project I spoke to many people who had known my father. I advertised in a Special Forces magazine, the *Drop*, and a paratrooper newspaper called the *Static Line*— both titles refer to parachute jumping. My phone began ringing after that. Men from all over the United States called me to tell me about my father — men who had known him as a nineteen-year-old paratrooper in the Second World War, men who had been stationed with him in Europe with the original Special Forces group, and men who fought with him in Vietnam. The stories poured in from letters and phone calls. They were full of names, connections, and memories. "One hell of a soldier," they all said. "A character, sharp, hard-nosed, great sense of humor." "Your dad was a hero," said Charles Petty, who fought at the Battle of the Bulge with my father. "You don't receive the Medal of Honor for nothing. I still think of your father often, and I have his photograph right here on my wall."

The first phone call came from a soldier who knew my father from their early days together in Germany. Sgt. Harry McGloughlin called one night after seeing my request for information. As I sat with my cordless phone on my deck under a night's sky of stars, I felt strangely like a daughter again and that this was my father on the other end. With a nervousness I had not anticipated, I ran for a pen and paper, not knowing where to begin with my questions. I also felt like the child who believed it was sacrilege to call a military man by his first name. I wasn't sure what to call him — Harry? Sergeant McGloughlin? Mr. McGloughlin?

His voice was the voice of a long-lost friend I didn't even know I knew or had missed until this moment. He was like family talking about the "old country." The strangeness of years melted as we spoke that night.

At the same time I recognized a defense I had carried around since childhood in the fortress: that kind of muscle-tightening defense I've always had when there's drink in the voice, stories on the edge. It's as if I've always been afraid of something exploding or the seams of life coming unraveled, knowing that the melting edges of lust and adventure and lightheartedness would never be able to put back together the lives of the men who surrounded my childhood. These men, like my father, lived as if perched on top of a mountain with one foot reaching for death across the way and that same grin my father wore on his face, as if he knew the dilemma of his life and chose to laugh.

To talk to Harry McGloughlin that night was to enter that world of the fortress again. I knew even as his voice came through the wires that there were no roads back from this journey, that from this night forward I risked opening up all that I had sealed up tightly. I risked knowing the men whom I had last seen at my father's funeral some twenty-three years before, and therefore I risked knowing my father. Little did I know then that the months ahead would roll into years and I would be adrift in time, extending my father's story into mine, photograph by photograph. Little did I know that the images he left behind would spark my own words and bring my past into my present.

But now I know that first phone call from Sergeant McGloughlin to the girl my father left behind to "carry on" was a chance happening between two strangers speaking in the night about a man they each once loved dearly. In discovering the loss of others who loved my father, I was to discover my own loss in ways I had buried. His call was a gift from the gods, one of many I would receive along my way.

He told me that he had seen my sister's request for information several years back but had felt at that time that we would be too young to hear what he had to say. But this time, he felt in his heart that it was indeed the time. He died a few months after that first phone call, neither of us knowing the seriousness of his illness at the time. The last time we spoke, I could tell from his fading voice that he was suffering greatly from his diabetes and heart trouble. I got off the phone and cried, and I wasn't sure why. I knew this soldier friend would someday take all the stories he had of my father to his grave. When he did die very soon afterward, I couldn't erase his address for the longest time from my address book, as if to do so was to erase the threads of my connection to my father. I had so wanted to tell this Harry, this sergeant, this Mr. McGloughlin that he helped push me on the path I needed to take.

And so began my steps into the unknown, my journey of a generation. What follows is a record of that journey, two journeys actually: the journey to find myself and the one to find my father. To understand him through the pictures he left behind, I had to come to the photographs as a little girl and as a daughter of a soldier, but also as a mother and a wife. Through the photographs, I hoped to find the place where all those pieces of myself came together.

Finding our fathers, like finding ourselves, is a journey we all take at one time or another — sometimes while our fathers are alive, and sometimes long after they have died. Sometimes during war, and sometimes during peace. The courage to reach back through time, to cautiously probe into the dark loam, mysteriously comes at some given moment as if dropped from the angels above.

Dreams

For weeks at a time I dream of fathers trying to reach their daughters. Over and over again in the night's land of sleep, my husband's father tries to call me on the phone. Fred, a friend from college, cries out to his daughter: "Andreita, Little Andrea," he calls. There is joy in his voice, tenderness in his calling. In the background of these dreams stands a colleague whose father left her money she uses for a writing program.

How does the world of my dead father reach the world of his living daughter, I wonder in the morning. Is it my writing that reaches up to my father, or is it he who touches my pen and moves it across the page?

Luella

My father is a serious child with his tiny turned-up nose and small, tightly closed lips. His face is round and sweet, and I can swear I've seen it before. I know those pudgy little hands, that indention under his mouth — I've seen the same piercing eyes in my two sons. What I

"Luella and baby Chas, date and place unknown."

can't see are the reasons my father would want to run away from his home someday, why he would hitchhike to Canada to fight in the Second World War.

My grandmother stands out clearly in this old sepia photograph, wearing a gauzy dress I might wear now. She looks nothing like she does today. It seems to me that she's always been old and this is a picture of someone else. She holds her baby with the same strength and confidence with which I've held mine. Her life and the life of baby Chas stretch past the point where the horizon comes into focus. It is a leap my mind is unable to make.

My grandmother turned one hundred years old on June 11, 1995. She still plays cards and can describe any event you want to know about. Since this photograph was taken, she's seen the death of her husband from cancer in the early 1950s, and she's seen the death of her oldest son from war. One of her best features remains her ability to move on, to find life and friendship where she can. She has long ago emptied out the attic of my father's old uniforms and other army paraphernalia and yet keeps one green beret in his childhood dresser. She places his photograph, the one she insisted he have taken before his last visit to Vietnam, on a living room table. She has learned to let go, like all those left behind must.

My father was not the first in his family to enter the army. This I know from Civil War documents framed and still hanging in my grandmother's house on New Street. My father grew up knowing this as well. His paternal grandfather, William Hosking, born in Red Ruth, England, enlisted from Hazel Green, Wisconsin, on October 2, 1861. At the age of twenty-four, he became a private in the Sixteenth Regiment Wisconsin Volunteer Infantry and served in the Civil War for three years. He was discharged in 1863 at Red Bone, Mississippi, and then reenlisted for three more years, fighting in the battle of Shiloh, Tennessee, the siege of Corinth, Mississippi, the siege of Atlanta, the March to the Sea, the battle of Columbia, South Carolina, and the battle of Bentonville. He was wounded by a minié ball and treated in a field hospital. Finally, he was honorably discharged on July 12, 1865, "by reason of the close of the war." His rheumatism, said in his obituary to have been caused by his war wound, bothered him for the rest of his life.

One of my father's maternal great-grandfathers, John Henry Luther, born in Saxony, Germany, enlisted from Wynaqua, New Jersey, on September 8, 1863. At the age of thirty-six, he was a private in the First Regiment of the New Jersey Light Artillery and served in many battles throughout the Civil War: Howletts House, Virginia, Clover Hill, Petersburg, Deep Bottom, Dutch Gap, and the fall of Richmond. Wounded by a shell in his left leg, he was treated in a camp hospital. At the close of the war he was honorably discharged and died twenty-five years later of heart disease, which a document my grandmother saved said he contracted while in the service.

I am surprised at how many battles these two immigrants fought and how long they both survived war. It reminds me of the guardian angel many have told me was with my father throughout his war experiences. People mention how often he came close to death, and how he managed to avoid it longer than anyone would have thought possible. Like the grandfathers before him, my father was to be discharged from the army, only to reenlist.

Before my grandmother married my father's father, she was engaged to a young West Point cadet now remembered only as LeRoy. They met while she was a nursing student in Poughkeepsie, New York, just up the Hudson River from West Point. When the cadets invited the group of young women to a dance, she and a friend took the ferry over. Eventually, my grandmother had her aunt make her a beautiful long dress for the dances. Her own mother was stingy with both her money and her love, so she dared not ask her, my grandmother tells me. My grandmother returned again and again to West Point not only because she loved dancing but because she fell in love with LeRoy. Eventually they were engaged and planned to marry, but the First World War came. He wanted to marry before he left for the war, but she said she wouldn't until he returned. Soon afterward he was killed in action somewhere in France.

Later, she married my grandfather Charles Ernest Hosking from Butler, New Jersey, who could never go to war because of his diabetes. They met at a party at a relative's home. Their second son was named Robert LeRoy. But it was their first son, Charles Ernest Hosking, Jr., who was destined for war.

Eighty years after LeRoy's death, my sister Janice, the poet of the family, wrote:

What were your dreams then, Grandma?
Dancing that night did you know you were holding
a ghost whose memory would be captured
in the name of another man's son?
Swirling, your cadet dies in France
in a war to end all wars.
Who would predict
that fifty years later you lose
another soldier in a country you know nothing about?
Would that seventeen year old

have danced long into the night
if she had known war would be so jealous
as to strike out twice against her?

1925

The Depression followed in the years after this posed childhood photograph was taken. It changed my father's generation forever and spilled over into the way he raised me. "Don't waste" became the slogan of my growing-up years with my father. "Turn off the lights when you're not using them. Don't throw out your food. Can't you reuse that somehow?"

I see my round-faced sons in this photograph, their blond hair combed neatly around their blue eyes. I see them sitting as protected as my father once was, and I wonder what lies ahead for them. I hear myself repeating lines sewn into my being: Don't waste. Don't ever waste your life, I want to tell them. Can't you reuse that somehow? Can't we make something beautiful out of the tragic?

Chas Hosking Jr., Brooklyn, New York

Standing next to a brick apartment house on the sidewalk of a tree-lined street in Brooklyn, my young father giggles and hangs his arms at his sides. A bow tie peers out through the top of his double-breasted coat. His legs are bare except for a pair of white anklets. He's come by himself on the train from New Jersey to visit Aunt Florence, the last of all my grandfather's siblings to still be alive. Uncle William, her husband, doesn't live with her anymore because he died aboard ship while headed for England in the First World War. In Brooklyn, my father has fun watching the same movie all day at the theater while Aunt Florence works, my grandmother tells me. He tells everyone about the cat who jumped out the fourth floor apartment window but survived. Like that cat, my father will have many lives, many close calls halfway around the world from this place.

For now he is a child who enjoys working in his grandparents' fields and selling the vegetables and strawberries at their roadside stand. He collects farming journals and says he wants to be a farmer someday. He raises rabbits in the backyard, saves string to wind into big balls, and puts rusty nails he hopes to use later into jars in the basement.

I gather from his school records that he had a noted high intelligence quotient but poor grades. He flunked high school plane geometry, English III, Spanish I, Latin II, and problems of democracy. He was excused from gym for health reasons three years in a row. A teacher rated his punctuality and personal appearance high but his initiative and personality low. He was absent from school for days at a time. The record mentioned that he wasn't at school enough his senior year to receive any marks. Home conditions were rated "medium" on a scale between excellent and poor, and no extracurricular activities were listed.

In the winter of 1938, my grandfather wrote to Aunt Florence, who had moved by then to Florida: "Charles has been very sick and is still a very sick boy; he goes to the doctor once a week for rheumatism of the joints — and his heart is bad after rheumatic fever. The poor boy tries so hard in school, but isn't getting much ahead. And he has his heart set on being a veterinarian doctor." Little did anyone know then that what my restless father really wanted was to quit school, leave home, and join the army.

I look at this boy and I vaguely see the man, but then it passes and I'm left with fragments of the man-to-be embedded in a small frame. He poses now as a carefree child in Brooklyn, and I see him at once on the Champs-Elysées in Paris, in front of the main Buddhist pagoda in Saigon, or standing at attention in a park in Southampton, England, with his three young daughters standing alongside him like a supporting cast. I look again at his face, and I see part of my brother, parts of my two sons, part of myself. But I don't see where his childhood dreams went to.

My soldier father asked to be cremated when and if he should die in Vietnam. My mother thought maybe it had to do with his new life among Buddhists. My grandmother thought he was crazy and in the end refused to let that happen. I think being cremated to my father meant that he would never be tied to one place but rather scattered to the four winds the way he lived his life. Perhaps it meant to him that no one could own him in the end and that he was a free man who could not be reclaimed as my grandmother wanted. If he couldn't be cremated, then he wanted to be buried in Arlington with those who knew him best, the tribe of the military. That was where he was rooted, not in an ancestral burial plot next to his family, where my grandmother insisted the army deliver his body.

The Generations

The two boys in this photograph, my Uncle Bob and my father, are now grandfathers themselves, and it is my two sons who could stand in their place. My older son, blond, serious, and taller than his younger brother, looks like my father here. My younger son, with something in his hands and a laugh on his face, could be my uncle. New grass has replaced the grass of my father's time, and new trees have replaced the old ones. Only now I am the parent posing next to the two sons the way my grandfather does here.

I know little about my grandfather since he died the month I turned twenty months old. I know he was the youngest child of parents who had both been married before but who had lost their first spouses. His father, a tin miner and mail carrier, had been born in Cornwall, England. His mother, Wilhemina Luther, came from Saxony, Germany, in time for her father to fight in the Civil War.

I know my grandfather through the stories I'm told — how tickled he was to have a granddaughter, how he spent every penny he had on things for me when he visited us in Fort Campbell, how it seemed he could never get enough of holding me. He was often ill with such things as diabetes, bad varicose veins, or a broken nose or rib from his boxing matches. He had to watch his diet and ate whole oranges, skin and all, for a vitamin C remedy for the varicose veins. He played the tuba in a music group before he married and went to secretarial school in the days when only men did that. He got a job running an office for a New York City steamship company, and because of that he and my grandmother sometimes got free rides to places along the East Coast.

"Charles E. Hosking Sr., Robert LeRoy, and Charles Jr."

In spite of often being sick, he loved being physical. He bought books on the latest exercises and learned judo, boxing, and wrestling. He worked out in the basement and continued jumping into the boxing ring until my grandmother threatened that it was either her or the ring. When my uncle's friend Howard Pitts came over in high school to visit, he would ask, "Mr. Hosking, can you show me another wrestling hold?" and they would commence to rolling on the living room floor with my grandmother nearby yelling that someone's foot might go through the radio in the corner. It is the same conversation I have nightly when my wrestling son, David, rolls on the floor trying to pin his father down in a new hold he's just learned.

At night after work and dinner, my grandfather would read as he sat in a big overstuffed chair and listened to the large radio which stood in the corner of the room. He smoked his pipe, and the times when he sat on the front porch and smoked, he would throw the matches into the bushes until the day my grandmother found a pile of them.

During the Depression my grandfather didn't accept "relief" and got a job keeping the books for a government welfare agency in Ridgewood. Years later, he would recount scenes of once wealthy men driving up in expensive cars to collect relief money. He and my grandmother would fight every morning about money, my uncle recalls. "Those were difficult times," he said. "We couldn't even afford to pay Mr. Mallerstein, the milkman, for years, but he still kept delivering. He said we'd pay someday when we could."

Later, my grandfather got a job with the Dupont company in Kearney, New Jersey, as their timekeeper in the payroll department. He lied about his age to get the job, my uncle tells me. He was five years older than he told them. The question kept coming up at home about what he would do when he was legally ready for Social Security — how would that work? my grandmother kept wondering. Because he knew a great deal about boxing, wrestling, weight lifting, and judo, he was asked to train the Dupont watchmen in self-defense. The company put barbed-wire fences around their buildings because they were afraid of the Japanese and German spies from the submarines coming in at night along the New

Jersey shores. During the Second World War, Dupont was making bomber noses, and there were spies interested in Dupont's work.

My grandfather bought a second-hand Buick to drive to work. It was a large car, my uncle remembers, one with so much room in the backseat that you had footrests when you stretched your legs out. Later he sold the car and started taking a combination of trains and buses to get to Kearney. The plant closed down right after my grandfather died at age fifty-nine (on record as fifty-four) of cancer, and the company moved their headquarters to Wilmington, Delaware. He had a good friend from work whom my father and uncle called Uncle Lee. The family would drive down to Patterson to visit him on weekends.

After my grandfather died, a man from Ramsey named Bill Pellington came to buy his barbells, weights, and other gym equipment in the cellar. My grandmother was constantly tripping over it when she went downstairs to do laundry or get more food from the cellar's storage room. Bill's father owned a bar called Pellington's up on Route 17. After the navy, Bill played on a local football team and eventually joined what was then called the Baltimore Colts.

I know my grandfather by the history and exercise books he read which are still on my grandmother's bookshelves and stacked in her attic. I see the jars of nails he left behind in his cellar, his boxing bag still hanging nearby. I know him by the letters he wrote his sister with such details as what he ate for Christmas dinner or how much the cigars cost that his nephew bought.

What I never knew about my grandfather until I asked my uncle about him was that he had a furious temper and got angry easily. My uncle remembers being spanked often and listening to my grandfather yell when he was angry. It had always looked to me from the photographs of my grandfather that he was the sensitive one and my grandmother was the family's hard edge. "Yes, it's true," my uncle says, "but even so, he did have a temper."

Album pages will turn one day, and my grandchildren who aren't even born yet will ask me as I now ask my grandmother, "Who's this, Grandma?" They'll want to know all about those who are no longer alive, just as I do. I will say old-fashioned things to them like "I rarely get out my good pocketbook anymore," and if they're like me, they will think it doesn't matter anyway. They'll worry when I don't get to the phone on time, and when I do, they'll ask me to tell stories about things I've forgotten. The names Aunt Radie and Cousin Lulu May, people from my father's childhood, will sound like characters out of a book, but I'll remember my father once told me they lived on Cherry Lane. My grandchildren who don't know me yet and will never know my father or grandfather will point to the Buddha necklace my father sent from across the ocean once, and I'll tell them about love's gifts, and time tumbling like a windswept meadow I once saw in Idaho. The thread toward my grandfather will be just that much longer.

Sailor on a Park Bench, Date Unknown

f I didn't take the time to study this photograph, I would miss that it is my father, for I think of him in an army uniform and not a navy one. This must have been taken during his short stint with the United States Coast Guard after having tried first to join the First Black Watch of the Canadian army. He had run away from home in 1941 before graduating from high school — had hitched a ride on a truck heading for Montreal on Route 17. Some vacationing family friends spotted my father in a Montreal bar and told my grandparents, who at that time had no idea where my father was. With the help of their congressman, J. Parnell Thomas, my grandparents got my father discharged a month after he enlisted. He ran away again, only to be stopped by border guards. This time he joined the Coast Guard reserves at age seventeen with the permission of my grandfather and then spent his time patrolling the beaches looking out for Japanese and German spies trying to come ashore.

In December 1942, the Coast Guard discharged my father because he had rheumatic heart disease with mitral stenosis. Still determined to join the army, he got help from his congressman to "pass" the physical and was inducted into the United States Army on May 1, 1943, eleven days before his eighteenth birthday. A year later, he left for Europe as a paratrooper.

Only now, as a mother of two sons, do I ponder the reasons why he ran away from home. I wonder about family dynamics, self-esteem, anger — those psychological terms of the 1990s. I wonder about loss — how a family of four experiences a sudden shift of space, changing from a square to a triangle. I search their faces in early family photographs for an explanation. Sometimes I see a somber tension, but my question isn't answered. My uncle tells me my father just wanted to fight in the Second World War, that he had gotten the "fighting bug" and would not rest until he was a soldier. When my oldest son tells me he might join the army someday, I feel myself cringing, the muscles around my heart tightening as if I am already preparing for his soldier death.

In a letter written by my grandfather on Christmas night, 1949, he writes to his sister: "You know Charles. He is so restless. It seems like he is no longer one of us. He has been away so long. Guess we will both be gone when he finally decides to come home to stay."

It looks as though this photograph was once in someone's wallet for quite some time. The paper is peeling from the back. There are cracks in it, tiny pieces actually missing, like the pieces of my father's story. Pieces I worry I will never find.

A Soldier's Album

pen any soldier's photo album and you will find this same picture: a young man with tender skin, posing in his first uniform, creating the illusion of maturity. He suddenly looks like the young soldier next to him, and one soldier album begins to look like all soldier albums.

My father had turned eighteen the month before on an army base in Mississippi, where he was becoming a soldier. He struggled through the rigorous training for which boot camp is famous. It was one thing to want to be a soldier; it was another to deal with physical exhaustion, homesickness, fear, and strict regulations.

He came to Camp Shelby as an individual, and he left as a member of a group. He lived with this group, and they became his family. Somewhere at the end of this evolutionary process, I imagine my father believed his possible soldier death in certain circumstances would be right. As another soldier wrote, it freed him to taste life.

"Camp Shelby, June 1943."

Somewhere packed in a box lies a photograph of myself at this
same age. My head tilts in the same direction as my father's, and
we look very much alike. Except I'm in a high school graduation
gown, something my father never wore. He had headed for life as
a soldier at the same age I headed north to college with the insur-
ance money from his death.

On Leave with George Martino
from Newark, New Jersey

The Saturday afternoon of March 18, 1944, finds PFC George Martino and my father having their picture taken in Lumberton, North Carolina. Outside, the dogwood buds are ready to explode, leaving the Tar Heel State a mass of pink and white.

In only a matter of time, my father will be shipped out to Europe, Allied troops will land in Normandy to invade northern France, and U.S. paratroopers will be dropped behind German lines to capture bridges and railroad tracks. German troops will surprise the Americans in the Ardennes Forest in Belgium, and the Americans, after two weeks of fighting, will stop them near the Meuse River, but not before 90,000 Americans are killed, wounded, or captured. History books will write about it as the Battle of the Bulge because of the battleground's bulging shape on the map.

It will be here in the month of December that my father's airborne group, the 509th, will be almost wiped out. After the war, it will exist no more. My father will be wounded the day after Christmas and sent to Atlantic City to recuperate in one of the old hotels along the ocean the military will take over for convalescent centers. My grandmother will want to take the train to visit him, but as she makes her way down New Street to the station, she will see him walking toward her on crutches.

Southern France, 1944

"Some baker," my father writes on the back of a photograph, taken behind Company B's sixty-mortar position in southern France. My nineteen-year-old father holds six loaves of bread in his arms and laughs as if there's no war going on. The sun shines over the French Maritime Alps and disguises the war. It won't be the last time his photographs will do that.

The view looks out toward Italy near Turini, France. The 509th Parachute Infantry Battalion is divided up in this part of Eu-

World War II parachutes. U.S. Army photograph.

rope – some in Italy at Lido-di-Roma, some fighting Germans in Le Muy, France, some riding through Cannes to liberate the city.

My father writes "some of the boys, 1944" on the back of another photograph from this time. He also writes that Charles Petty sits at the far right of the picture. At age twenty-eight, Petty acts as an older brother to my father, who joined the 509th, Company B, Third Platoon as a replacement. After some time in the Maritime Alps, the company headed north to Paris. I find this out forty-eight years later when I speak to Petty long distance in California. My sister Janice came across his telephone number somehow and gave it to me. On the phone he recalled, as if it were yesterday, how he had wanted to attend Christmas mass at Notre Dame cathedral, but the 509th was called to the Battle of the Bulge right before he was ready to leave. Company B's job was to hold open the Hotten-Soy Road. Petty went out on patrol, and my father was inside a machine gun emplacement dug in near the German line. When Petty returned, he tells me, he sat on a pile of sugar beets eating stew from a can of C rations and watching the snow fall. Someone yelled, "Hosking's been wounded!" A shell in the chamber of my father's .45 pistol had accidentally discharged, shattering parts of my father's leg. It wasn't easy to pull him out of the dugout, Petty tells me, because he had to be dragged out through trenches that were in full view of the Germans. Petty ran up as they gave my father first aid and waited for the ambulance. He remembers the grin on my father's face in spite of his wounds and his saying as they took him away: "You think things will get worse, Petty, before they'll get better?"

In the same month the Battle of the Bulge began in Belgium, my grandfather wrote his sister on Christmas Day:

We received three or four letters from Charles Jr., about thirty days ago together with half a dozen pictures — small ones taken somewhere in the mountains of southern France. Not fancy ones. But showing them just as they were — in battle dress, armed to the teeth, and making a meal outside a mountain home. Looked like stew, or something they were making; pouring water out of a gasoline tin. A boy in one picture was holding a wine bottle — probably empty. And a goat was in one picture. Maybe they were making goat stew! Anyhow, they all looked good — and tough — but, nevertheless, rather seedy and forlorn looking. I am only praying that they are all right since this new battle is raging in France. One of Charles' friends from Ramsey who was in the same outfit with Charles, wrote his mother that he had been wounded five times; is now in the hospital again and that out of his entire company that was shipped from Camp McCall, North Carolina, only three are now alive, he being one of them. Charles never tells us anything. I hope Charles is one of the three. If this war would only get over, we would all feel better.

In the same letter, my grandfather wrote that "victory or defeat may be the end of a fight — the ultimate outcome naturally — but the real fun, the real enjoyment, or the real despair can come only while fighting, not after the bugle blows; and that those who have had to fight and fight hard, whether it be a fight against disease, poverty, or death can attest to that."

As I read my grandfather's letter, I jump ahead to a photograph taken in Vietnam in May 1965 while my father was on an aerial reconnaissance. He and Sergeant Jones fly in a helicopter called a UTT above the Saigon River in Tay Ninh Province. I wonder if it's from up this high that my father gained an awareness of life. While some soldiers grew addicted to drugs in Vietnam, did my father get hooked to adrenaline and being on the edge? Had the army from the beginning habitually drawn him in, offering him a way to live and a way to die?

I imagine nothing in ordinary peacetime kept my father in a state where all his senses were alive — a constant reminder that now was all he had. It was simple and primal. No wonder his transition to home was an impossibility. He knew early on that life didn't owe us time. Perhaps he remained in the army after his first war so he would always be with those who knew what he had seen in war.

I read from a young soldier's diary in J. Glen Gray's book *The Warriors: Reflections of Men in Battle* that one is never the same after war. "I cannot face the prospect of going back to any of my old haunts after the war. I shall not want to speak of these war years, and I cannot be as I was. What is left?"

Mother's Day, 1944

I recall that while in Vietnam, my father always remembered our birthdays and Christmas. Far from home, he even acknowledged Mother's Day. That in itself is not particularly notable except that given the war environment he was in without any familiar external clues, he kept an internal clock for the ones he loved. Of course, as an adolescent, I expected that. I wasn't surprised when a gift arrived wrapped in delicate paper from so far away. It is only now that I recognize what lengths he had to go to keep a schedule of our lives in his heart.

During my father's first war experience, he wired two dozen roses from Italy to his mother for Mother's Day, 1944. It was a beautiful May afternoon when they arrived. They were a gift so luxurious that my grandmother wanted to remember them forever. She brought her grandmother's pedestal outside and draped a fringed cloth over it. Then she placed on it a round blue vase full of the deep red roses and lovely ferns. Someone took a photograph that afternoon as the sun opened up the buds and the flowers looked upward to the blue sky.

For a moment as I look at the photograph now over half a century later, I imagine the tears in my grandmother's eyes, the joy revealed on her face as she took in a deep breath of her favorite flower. With each breath she inhaled, she remembered her first-born child and prayed he would return from war. For years afterward, she planted roses in her yard, and when they bloomed she filled the vases on her tables with their fragrance. She took care of her rosebushes until she could no longer bend down to trim their branches. My sister Betty Ann took over the tradition then and now plants rosebushes in her own yard. She takes care of the roses like a sacred garden whose beauty reaches back across the decades, across an ocean, across a schedule of our lives.

Norman, 1945

1945 was a busy year: Hitler died in Berlin, Germany surrendered unconditionally to the Allies, the Second World War ended in Europe, and we dropped the atomic bomb on Hiroshima and Nagasaki. My father came home to rest after the war and got together with his friend Norman Stegan. They posed on a bench in the front yard for my grandfather. My father wore a T-shirt with the word PARATROOPER written across the top, and his dog tags, which he will wear every day for the rest of his life, hung around his neck. As my grandfather snapped the picture, my father told Norman about his experiences in the war. He didn't want to talk about sports or school anymore. It was clear that the army had already become his life.

While my father was home resting, they double dated some of the local girls and reminisced about working together at the O'Mahoney Feed Company out on Darlington Avenue where they first met when my father was in high school. Norman had been the truck driver then, and my father had worked in the mill or helped Norman with the deliveries. Years later, Norman was to write me from his retirement in Florida that my father was a happy-go-lucky kind of guy, a practical joker with a smile on his face. He used to mimic the boss and make Norman laugh. Their friendship grew even as their lives separated.

Norman and my father eventually married and had children.

Each time my father came home to Ramsey between his stationed army tours, they got the families together and talked about how proud they were of their children, Norman wrote me. Norman became Ramsey's chief of police, and we lived in Europe, where my father parachuted out of airplanes, carried a heavy rucksack through the Alps, and practiced war. When my father was forty-two, they met again in Ramsey, only this time they didn't speak. This I recall from memory: Norman leads the parade of cars from the Van Emburgh Funeral Parlor down Main Street and makes his way to the old Dutch Reformed Church graveyard in Paramus, where my father is buried in a family plot near Revolutionary War soldiers. Under Norman's command, the entire police department volunteers to lead the funeral procession. They stop traffic as the long line of cars, some with flags whipping in the wind, solemnly follow one behind the other. We enter the gates of the old graveyard and follow the police to my father's final resting spot.

Physical Training

Somewhere between the beacon and the barracks at Fort Benning, Georgia, my father does the push-ups he did every day for the rest of his life. I remember as a little girl thinking he could do more push-ups than anyone. Sometimes he looked serious when he straightened his back and legs to an even slant and then lifted his arms up and down, as if he were doing penance. Other times, he laughed self-consciously and blushed as I watched him.

My father, like his father before him, believed in the value of physical strength. He skied, climbed mountains, swam, and did simple basic training exercises over and over again. He didn't smoke, and I don't even remember him taking an aspirin because, as he said, it might hurt his body. He prided himself on being stronger than many of the new recruits. "Don't ever smoke, Gail. You see what it does to even these young men," he said to me. His body was a tool he knew could make the difference between life and death someday.

During a phone conversation, Al Arellano, a man from New Mexico who joined the army at age fifteen, said that my father was

September 7, 1946, Fort Benning, Georgia.

an old soldier. "He would tell Second World War stories and do push-ups and sit-ups before daylight. He was a physical training fanatic and quite disciplined. I thought the world of him. Guys like your dad made me stay in the army. He was a character!" Then with a pause and a laugh, Al remembered an incident from the 1950s at the barracks in Lenggries, Germany, after my father wrecked his car one snowy winter night. "Your dad must have gone off the road and landed in the river and then just left the car there. He came back to the barracks soaked — he had swam across the cold river. He hid in the barracks until the MPs showed up. 'Hoskins in this unit?' the MPs asked. 'Where is he?' When they left he came up from the basement still soaking wet, laughing that he had just done E&E [escape and evade]."

Mike O'Connor calls me with the same story but adds that my father "was wasted" that night. He doesn't mention that drinking was the one way my father did not take care of his body. He tells me instead that my father always kept several sets of car keys in case someone took one away from him. "We put your dad on a bunk in the barracks until the MPs came back the next morning to take him home and to identify the car. Captain Smith gave him an article fifteen as a disciplinary action instead of him getting court martialed. People always protected your father. Maybe because he was such a good soldier."

June 30, 1948, Textile Hall, Columbus, Georgia

'd like to say my father looks happy here next to his friend Arnett as they each pose with a beer in hand at a local club. But as I look at this photograph many times, I notice that I can't be sure. Perhaps the look on my father's face just reveals that it's too hot this summer afternoon outside Fort Benning. Or maybe he's tired from teaching men to jump off of 250-foot towers into the swirling wind at the Parachute Infantry Training School. Or maybe this master parachutist has just lost his patience with all the newcomers. I don't know. I have no exact notion of that day back in 1948, just months away from my father meeting my mother and two years before I will be born. Yet I feel as if I've been to this club like any of the enlisted men's clubs I've seen in other times and places. Someone puts a few coins in the jukebox and a song like "It's Magic" fills the noisy hall. One beer becomes two beers and so on until the spirit loosens. This was who my father was some of the time: just an ordinary GI drinking some beers far from home. Some of the time he didn't know when enough was enough, and he was oblivious to responsibilities. But to stop there isn't to know the whole man. It would be to ignore his deep sense of duty, his working as if every detail mattered. It would be to forget the soldier who wanted the world for his family. The soldier who would one day save the lives of his comrades.

Love and Marriage

y father on furlough, home in August 1948, posed in his front yard with a girlfriend named Audrey. She was a local girl, my uncle told me when I asked him about her. There are several photographs of her in my father's album, one even of my grandfather with his arm around her waist. Maybe the family thought they might marry, but my uncle has no recollection of that. Other women are in my father's albums too. Women I never met. Pretty women with red fingernails, jewelry around their necks, and curls. They smile, and I wonder if they thought of love with my father — or marriage? There was Juanita in Winston-Salem, Jeanne while on furlough in 1944,

Kentucky, 1950.

Emily in 1945, and then a beautiful stranger at the Rainbow Roof of the Ansley Hotel in Atlanta in August 1948.

Only eight months later, in April 1949, my father drove to New Jersey with my mother to meet my grandparents, who knew nothing of their sudden marriage. Captured on my parents' arrival from Georgia, where it was legal for a sixteen-year-old girl to marry, were my mother's curls, thick with youth, and my father's grin, the one I saw whenever he showed real joy. I imagine my father saw in my mother a quiet beauty, someone sensitive and loving and ready to follow him anywhere. My mother, I imagine, saw a hero who could take her away from a place with no future. She saw him as a charming man who knew what he wanted.

Theirs was a love that fired up quickly and then often smoldered as they got to know each other. "I thought I loved you," my father said to her on their honeymoon in Georgia. My mother had locked herself in the bathroom and was crying. I think life with a man came all too quickly for her. She was still a girl, and was frightened. Later, when I came along, she said nothing made her happier.

"Such innocence," a friend of mine remarked when I showed her a photograph taken in 1950 of my mother age seventeen, my father age twenty-six, and me just a baby. We were beginning our lives together and had no clues to the future. Nor did anyone tell us that military life is not a life for the innocent. War, military reviews, patriotism, and monuments to fallen warriors are not conducive to family life. For all the camaraderie my father shared as a "soldier's soldier," he struggled with how to be with my mother.

I can't deny that my father was not a good husband. He was torn between leaving and retrieving the family he seemed to want so much. He lacked tenderness with my mother and spoke to her too authoritatively. Looking back I see that most of the time his needs took precedent over hers. My mother's needs were simple. She only wanted from my father love, his company, and a recognition of what it was like to live with a soldier. My father's needs were more complex, those of a man struggling with demons and an ideal. Theirs became a relationship of opposites and incompatibility.

In a photograph taken of my parents near our Fort Bragg apartment in October 1952, I see that my father stands behind my mother and holds her shoulders as though he loves her very much but can't be sure what that means. I imagine him wanting to squeeze her — partly in anger because she wasn't all he hoped for, and partly with a deep love he never felt for anyone else. I see him positioning her toward the world the way he wanted everyone to see her: dressed in the clothes he chose and smelling of French perfume that he bought for her at the Post Exchange. He wanted my mother to face the world head on and take care of everything he couldn't, like the children and the life at home. My father couldn't give what was demanded of a family man. Slowly he broke my mother's heart and then her spirit.

From my mother I gathered a sense of the humble, the quiet, the gentle touching of skin. I learned about women friends, brightly painted toenails, and leaving one's family to follow the man you love. From her I witnessed loneliness, buried words, okra and fried chicken dinners.

From my father I learned to admire adventure, foreign words, and spicy foods. I learned to love books and to treasure them above all. I witnessed his code of details, discipline, and duty, swallowing them like a hungry baby bird.

Shopping in a store, my mother might spend hours choosing just the right thing as if it might be her only chance in life to purchase anything. My father, on the other hand, would know exactly what he wanted and buy it quickly before he changed his mind and his old Depression guilt about spending any money returned to haunt him.

My parents left their homes behind when they married, never to return again — only visitors in a familiar but strange land. But in the end, each was buried down the road from their childhood homes, many states and hundreds of miles away from each other. The places they had wanted to leave behind became the places where their bodies were brought to rest. Their graves leave no clue of their ever having come together. Only the children they left behind can attest to that.

What my father did in his life with my mother was to take pictures and then organize them into albums as if we were on a straight line to the future. If my parents could have seen the future in its entirety, would they have appreciated their love for each other more? Would they have understood how much their struggles spilled over into their children's lives? Might they have danced more tenderly in the time left to them?

Company F, 503rd AIR,
Fort Campbell, Kentucky, 1951

A uniformed soldier pays close attention to details as he polishes my father's Buick until it shines. The one-story, white army barracks behind him look familiar to me. They could be on any army base I've lived on. I've seen soldiers walking from one assignment to the next outside similar rows of wooden buildings. The American flag waves above them no matter what base it is and leaves a shadow over the unpaved space between the buildings. The telephone poles weave a line of wire into the distance, going out to the places from where these men have come.

Here the soldiers live, doing work that is at once specific and nebulous: prepare these potatoes, clean these weapons, file these papers, fix that jeep, drive this over to the motor pool, or shine these boots. I can imagine that the details make sense for the moment, but somewhere in the middle of a march, before the left foot touches the ground, one's mind might wander and then wonder why one is at an army base on this particular day doing this particular work. What is this war we are here to prevent? Just what is a soldier's work for?

For those so intricately involved with details, there is an unspoken sense in the army that everything is ephemeral: friendships, peace, even my father's life. Time is never an uninterrupted continuum. It is fragmented with TDY (temporary duty) assignments, or even the so-called permanent duty, which is never more than three years. Ancient buildings can be destroyed in a morning of bombs, and men can be called in the middle of the night to gather their gear and prepare for war. The thought of death lingers over any army camp.

Simone Weil wrote in 1940 after the fall of France that the relationship between death and the future is different for soldiers than for other men. For the civilian, death is a limit on life in the future, but for the soldier death is the future. "It is the profession's assignment."

In the end, every soldier knows what the author of *The Iliad* knew thousands of years ago:

Yet even I, like you, must someday encounter my fate,
whether the hour strikes at noon, or evening, or sunrise,
the hour that comes when some arms-bearing warrior will
kill me.

Into Focus

My tiny hand rests on the same watch I remember my father wore all the time. As my grandfather and mother look into the camera, my father stares down at me with a smile on his face. I don't have many photographs of him holding me, but in all of them we look like we belong together, with our blond hair and similar faces. He holds me in this photograph as if he is comfortable with his baby daughter. But I have no recollection of his touch, no memory of his skin. I have only a visual impression of tattooed arms.

Much is unspoken in this photograph. My mother's pregnancy shows no visible clues to me, nor does the cancer that will kill my grandfather the same month my sister is born. There are no signs telling us that in two months my father will severely injure his legs during a routine training mission. The future General Westmoreland, the soldier he will meet again on a jeep in Vietnam, will be observing. When he runs over to my father and asks, "Soldier, are you all right?" my father, with his usual sense of humor, will look down to check all his body parts and then say, "Yes Sir!" My mother will call my grandparents, begging them to return to Fort Campbell, where my father will spend months in the hospital and a year healing. By the time he is well, he will be too old for the officer-training opportunity his superiors recommended.

It is difficult as I look at my father's photographs to bring his powerlessness into focus. It is at odds with the image he projected for so many years, another mask he wore in our presence. I took his confidence at face value, just as life in the fortress insisted on being taken. This illusion of perfection and invincibility he carried around became second nature to me as well. As the years went by I struggled with letting go of this notion. I was terrified of being left bare without the mask my father had shown me.

Roots and Vines

Representatives from four generations of a family stand on the land my great-grandfather Gilbert gave my grandparents for a wedding present: my great-grandmother Fanny Bartholf, Grandma Hosking, my father, and me. Now I know, but didn't as a child, that my father's roots go back even farther on this New Jersey soil. My ancestors came from Holland, Germany, Scotland, and England as early as the 1600s, people like Gulliaem Bertholf, one of America's first Dutch Reformed ministers and affectionately called "Dominae" by many; Henrik Bertholf, a prosperous farmer; and a family named Ramsey from Scotland. They settled in places named by the native Americans who were there when they arrived: Mahwah, meaning "smiling fields"; Pompton, meaning "place where they catch the soft fish"; and Wyckoff, meaning "high ground." They took their produce to places like Washington Island Market in Paterson or to New York to the Gansevoort Market at the foot of 14th Street. They navigated their horses and wagons over dirt and then cobblestone roads.

Although my father had roots that dug deeply into America, I often felt there were no roots in our life, only thin vines growing on the soil we happened to be stationed on that year. Because his life was one of constant moving, like a nomad in search of a place, so was mine. Whenever I am asked now, "Where are you from?" I say, "My father was in the army," as though that is an explanation of place. At other times I say, "Everywhere and nowhere," shrugging it off as if I don't know where to begin. It is always an awkward question which reveals to me instantly my sense of rootlessness. That delicate balance of outsider and insider still tips one way and then the next after all these years.

As I look at this picture of the generations I wonder how my children will partake of the memory of the family stories I've heard, like the one about my great-grandparents' wedding, when the minister and Great-Grandpa Gilbert arrived late on horseback to Fanny's home. My children never knew them, and already I'm careless about the particulars I've heard. I ask my grandmother if the wedding was in October, when I imagine the winds still blowing warm and leaves rustling in their color. No, it was February, she answers, when the snow was above the first-floor porch. What other times have I lost, like Gilbert losing the box with his wedding suit in it somewhere between Fardale Avenue and Airmont Avenue. No one found the suit until the spring, my grandmother tells me. Soon she will be gone, and I will be the one who must pass on the family memories. I fear losing them, like time piling scraps I no longer recognize into a corner.

The natural successive link to these stories would have been my father, but now that he's gone that won't happen. My children never knew my father. How will they make that leap over generations? It's as if I must represent my father's generation before I'm allowed to designate my own. Item by item, I ask my grandmother questions about the past. I want to get the dimensions right; I must be the missing link. I scurry to collect memories before the earth swallows them up as though they never existed.

June 2, 1952, Smoke Bomb Hill, Fort Bragg, North Carolina

My father looks awkward in the role of caretaker. I can almost hear him say to my mother as he holds my baby sister Janice in this photograph: "Hurry up and take the picture so you can take over." He sits on a blanket on a Fort Bragg field and holds Janice with caution as if he is afraid he will drop her. In spite of his not knowing exactly what to do with his baby girls, who come every eighteen months until there are three of us, he packs us into the car and insists on picnics and summer drives. It is a scenario he will repeat all our lives together. Like the outline of a plot, he will give us particulars to remember as he insists we see as much of the world together as we can.

I never doubted my father's pride in us, but I remember his helplessness in being the father of females. He grew up with one brother and then spent the rest of his life in the company of men. He was often clumsy with us and unnecessarily authoritarian. His high standards were meant for soldiers, not daughters. Raised on an idealism that perfection was possible, we were destined to internalize his model and struggle forever to find an elusive middle ground.

In another photograph taken near the Chiemsee in Bavaria, my father looks like he is threatening us one more time about our uncontrolled childish ways — our bouncing in the car, our running ahead, our loud voices in the spring air. He had a need for quiet, for clean, inspected bedrooms, for children to wear slippers in the house at all times. He would raise his voice, not ever his hand, and I would feel frightened each time. I dared not tell him of mistakes. "Don't tell your father," my mother would say, which only added to my fear. I tiptoed around him, trying to sense his mood, trying to meet his expectations.

Once for Father's Day when I was eleven, I refused to buy him a present because, as I told my mother, he didn't deserve it. In our small kitchen in building 106, my father told me he heard why I didn't get him a present. I was embarrassed, and large, hot tears streamed down my face. He said only, "You are right, Gail. I know I'm not always so gentle with you girls. I am used to dealing with men all day and I forget when I'm home that you are little girls, not soldiers. I'm sorry."

Years later, when I sat in a Writing about War workshop and read this story out loud, I looked up to see tears in the eyes of the two retired men, both veterans, sitting across from me at the table. "You know, Gail," one of them said, "there aren't many men who would apologize to an eleven-year-old girl with such honesty."

Gail and I

How many times have I seen this photograph? Only now with careful study late at night do I find what French philosopher Roland Barthes calls the "punctum" — that tiny hole in a photograph that lets me step through to the other side, piercing my heart with the truth of what the chemicals developed.

The truth is found in the way my face lights up and I hold my

August 1952, Fardale, New Jersey.

small arms around my father's head. The way my chin rests into his army regulation haircut, the one I suddenly remember, its feel still tickling my hand.

This is my daddy, the photograph seems to be saying, as if my two-year-old frame can speak through the image risen to the paper's surface. Loud and proud and unencumbered with the past or the future.

My father writes "Gail and I" on the back, and I feel its clarity of single relationship for the first time. I know without a doubt that the bonds of first love never truly let you go. How smitten I am here, and for a second just now I remember his wide hand holding my wrists, my feet dangling on his chest, and the crisp feel of his khakis.

Betty Ann, September 1953, Fort Bragg

My sister arrived as one of the so-called army brats born in Womack Army Hospital in June 1953. She went from the army hospital to the army dependents' housing, where we lived side by side with other enlisted men's families. Each building was the same, as was the life-style of those inside. To live there was to live in a home within a fort and guarded gates surrounding the entrances. We grew up therein, riding our bikes and playing as naturally as if it were the tree-lined street of a small town, as if every child in America watched men jump out of planes or march by with heavy rucksacks.

When I drove past these same apartment buildings as an adult, I was surprised to find that they stood exactly as in 1953. Nothing had changed. The grass still needed watering and the bushes were still thin. Outside each apartment, dozens of small children played, some in small plastic swimming pools with mothers sitting nearby on lawn chairs. The absence of men was striking, and I suddenly remembered the loneliness of wives on army bases. Every couple of years there would be a new base, a new apartment, a new group of women and children to meet as the men continued their familiar comings and many goings. I remembered crying each time my father's new orders came. I never truly got used to saying good-bye.

It was the army itself, the foundation of familiar communities like this one, that kept me from feeling like a complete immigrant once. Suitcases in our hands and dog tags around our necks, my family packed up often for new places with familiar expectations and routines. The terms were always the same — the snack bar, the PX, the commissary with its discounted foods, the dispensary, men marching, men leaving, everyone on alert. Is it no wonder decades later I find myself inviting immigrants home for dinner?

Looking normal is the mask an army base uses to survive. The children playing, the woman in coffee klatches, and the mailman delivering mail hide what a stranger might see if he entered one of those doors. For it is only inside that one sees what the life of a soldier's family is really like. Part of the confusion, part of the job of both the soldier and his family, is submitting to the unavoidable necessity of leaving. One's mind is always tuned to the world's events, wondering just when the soldiers will leave home again. All the while, as Bill warns Sally in John Van Druten's 1945 play *The Voice of the Turtle*, "You mustn't ask a soldier what the war's about." What pumps through every military family's veins is the fear of which direction history will take and the question of where it will leave us in its squeeze.

Once during the Iraqi War, when many American soldiers were coming home, a crowd of their families gathered at a nearby park to welcome them back. I was standing on a friend's porch that morning when another friend came up and referred to the gathering crowd in the park. "Isn't it disgusting that they're all there?" she asked, with no idea why anyone would care to be there on the soldiers' arrival. The other friend agreed and then mentioned that during the Vietnam Parade in Washington her veteran brother-in-law cried as the troops went by. "He is still talking about that war! Can you believe it?" she said. I was speechless and felt the ground under me suddenly split. Politics and propriety aside, I knew, as army brats know, what that crowd knew — that all they truly wanted was to hold again that person who had left with rifle in hand for a foreign place, none of us knowing if he would ever return. Who shall live and who shall die, the ancient question asked on each Jewish New Year, is what haunts each and every member of that gathering crowd in the park. This every army brat knows by heart.

At Captain Smith's

My father loved a shiny new automobile. Lots of his free time was spent keeping its luminescent look as he polished the chrome with a chamois cloth. I don't remember ever seeing our car dirty. But I do remember that he wrecked many of them and that he lost rank stripes as a consequence. My mother got out her sewing box then, clipped the old stripes, cleaned off the threads, and waited for the next promotion. The accidents occurred when he drank, and I was told he was lucky to be alive afterward. Time after time his guardian angel let him walk away untouched.

The camera from so long ago captured my father's drinking

eyes and my memories of those unpredictable times. He might smile more freely and joke around but then not show up at an important event. He embarrassed us by coming late to my brother's baptism and swaying up the chapel's center aisle as I wanted to fade into the air. Sometimes he disappeared for days, off drinking in some German village, or he brought boisterous soldiers home to party with him. I wasn't sure who he was on those occasions. Here was my father, a serious man with rules and regulations and discipline, now let loose like a happy-go-lucky kid again. I was never sure which side of him wore a mask. Loud music and laughter blared in our apartment, and I would listen as he told stories to the gathered crowd. In the morning empty brown bottles and full ashtrays filled the table. Sometimes when I peeped into the living room, I would see a sleeping soldier or two. It was quiet, as if I had only imagined the party.

I learned early on about this disease of secrets — how it has the power to take love and confuse those in its grip, the power to change a personality, and the power to catch the rest of us off guard. Looking at this 1953 photograph, I see my civilian-dressed father standing in a familiar military "at ease" stance. It is this juxtaposition, this duality, that my father came in and out of his whole life: one in control and one out of control. I know from his eyes and his grin that alcohol had crept into his life by then. It wasn't daily. I recall he went long periods of time without drinking. Others have told me it never interfered with his work and that they "could always count on Snake." But the army made drinking easy with its discounted tax-free liquor and its institutionalized parties. When the alcohol appeared, it threw darts into our lives as it soothed his demons and kept his pain a private domain.

April 8, 1954, Berchtesgaden

Although this is a black-and-white photograph taken of my parents on a spring day many years ago standing alongside a rural road in Europe, I remember clearly the yellow sweater and tweed sports coat my father wears and my mother's beige winter coat with three round, smooth buttons. I feel as if I could lead anyone to find these familiar clothes in my parents' closets that don't exist anymore. I remember the clothes as if I had just put them away. Their texture, their color stay with me, not the memory of this particular day or the fleeting experience of my young parents in 1954. How is it that this remains so?

While writing this book, I have been struck again and again with something that appears so simple and yet haunts me. That is the fact that we don't know what lies around each bend of life. My parents in this photograph could not have begun to tell you what was next, just as I can't now. If our lives are like novels, they can only be fully written in retrospect. We are all short stories, written on the run — a collection of photographs, images that remain with us. Pieces of stories are always missing, always will be missing. We take some stories to our graves, and they disappear like the clothes my parents are wearing on this day in 1954. It is my writing that struggles to bring them back to life. Perhaps this is why I've become a writer — the collector of a lost world.

Summer 1954, Benediktbeuern

My father's starched summer khakis disturb the composure of this otherwise relaxed photograph taken in the German village of Benediktbeuern. His crisp uniform tucked into his laced-up black boots belongs inside the fortress, not near a summer's meadow. He places his hand on my shoulder, and I remember now its firm weight. I am four years old, the oldest of his three daughters, already aware of "behaving," ready to please.

I think about growing up seeing that only men can make a difference, watching men control the lives of women, and feeling invisible when my father is away so much. I watched women afraid to live with men and afraid to live without them. In the female military dependent's life, I learned to keep my guard up and not to question authority. A middle ground didn't exist.

I want now from the world of men what my mother could never have: to be taken seriously, to count as an equal, and never to be the invisible servant in the background. It is a delicate balance of male and female, duty and middle ground, the fortress and the

"Benediktbeuern, 1954, Janice, Betty Ann, and Gail."

civilian. I search out where each belongs and how I cross over from one world to the other. I want what was so difficult for my father — to be able to let go of the warrior and enter the world of meadows and children and summer afternoons.

My hand moves in this photograph probably because I didn't keep it still while my mother clicked the camera. Its movement is the punctum through which I enter and find the writer on the other side of this photograph, already jotting down my memories, already observing my father's world. From the days when I was surrounded by limits I push the boundaries with my pen now way beyond the mountains in Bavaria. My pen leads me back and forth from then to now, chasing time, moving the photograph's edges until they are out of sight.

It was my mother who first found this village when she was looking for a place to live with her three children while my father studied the Czech language in Oberammergau. Dependents' housing had not been built yet, and we were on our own "on the economy," as the military phrase went. She settled on some rooms just down the mountain path from Anna and Joseph Branhofer. Eventually they became our friends, and we referred to him as Uncle Zeppi. He and Anna had no children, so Janice's and my arrival every morning in our pajamas for breakfast amused and flattered them. We fed Uncle Zeppi's pet deer with a bottle and bathed in a hollowed-out log under tall pine trees in the Alps. We watched new guests arrive each week from the German film industry at his A-shaped Bavarian home. Uncle Zeppi's world became our world. My father would be gone for weeks at a time and then show up unexpectedly.

Thirty-five years later I return to this village and find Anna and Uncle Zeppi in another house in the same village. I am concerned they won't remember me, but suddenly as I sit at their table they bring out a thick album and open it to pictures of us all together. There I am as if it were yesterday pouring out *Orangesaft* into a glass at one of Uncle Zeppi's outdoor tables or standing naked in a hollow log with cold mountain water pouring over my sisters' backs. There I am twirling under an evergreen. Time is pinned down between the pages of these strangers I barely remember. Uncle Zeppi tells me that he is not surprised I am a teacher. I was teaching him English when I was five. "Das ist ein Loffel — this is a spoon," I'd say as I pointed to it on the table. When asked in those days where my father was, I replied, "He is in Ober-ober-gau." Already I did not question why my father always had to leave us.

After my father's schooling was finished and dependents' housing had been built in Bad Tölz, we moved to an apartment there. Sometimes on weekends we would drive back to Benediktbeuern, the village thick with the smell of "honey wagons" carrying manure out to the fields. Cows sometimes walked right down the middle of the narrow roads while my father stopped the car and waited for them to get out of the way. Houses were attached to barns, young girls wore aprons over their dresses, and young boys dressed in leather shorts and suspenders. We'd walk up the mountain to Uncle Zeppi's house and spend the afternoon feeding the deer and eating under the trees.

My father put another photograph into his album taken this same summer in Benediktbeuern. It isn't the picture of two Germans sitting outside a *Gasthaus* with Janice and me that catches my attention but rather that my father wrote "two Krauts" on the back. From the front of the picture I guessed these two people might have been friends from the way they tenderly surround us. The Second World War and all its ugliness flashes through here with my father's pen. It reminds me that the war is not over. It is this mistrust of appearances that I could not have had as a child but that my father must have learned in the theater of war. The child who became the woman/writer/teacher of this picture asks now, Where were they all, Uncle Zeppi as well, when the German soldiers shot at my father? Where were they all when the children I didn't have yet drove by in boxcars headed for their deaths? Where are the limits of tenderness?

Intelligence and Language School, Oberammergau

"Some people say your father was called the Snake because he was sly and quick to get out of difficult places," Harry McGloughlin said to me on the phone when we were talking about their studying together at the American Army Intelligence and Language School in Oberammergau. "But I know the real reason. Your father had a front bridge of false teeth because his front teeth had been knocked out once in a fight. When he drank, the bridge would sometimes slip, and he would spit like a snake. That's how it all started. Your mom called him Chuck, and his mother called him Charles, but we called him the Snake. People in Germany translated that into 'die Schlange,' and that made him angry. He never wanted his daughters to hear people call him that.

"Your dad was my good friend. He had a great sense of humor, but I think his exterior hid his deep sensitivity. He struggled with alcohol's power. He was like two different people, really. When he drank, the other person took over. Living on the brink of death does strange things to men, Gail. That's where your father lived as a soldier, always on the brink of death. In 1966, I saw him at Fort

Bragg before he left for his third hitch to Vietnam, and he told me
he wasn't coming back this time."

John Kingerter called me as well to talk about my father. "Your
dad was a very smart guy. Never a phony. Some of the guys called
him Snake, but we younger soldiers always called him Sergeant
Hosking. I saw your article in the *Army Times* magazine, and I
wanted to tell you how much I admired your dad. I knew him
back in the 1950s in Germany. He was one of the few older soldiers who would speak to us younger guys. We looked up to him.
He was outgoing but never played the political game. He called
things the way they were. Rank never scared him. Maybe that's
why he didn't get promoted as much. You might say he was a kind
of outlaw. Great soldier, though. He was an old-timer with that
old-fashioned patriotism you don't see anymore.

"You know, my daughter's twenty-three now. Her whole life
she's heard me say whenever she says something I can't relate to,
like, 'Dad, one of the Beatles died,' I always say, 'Who cares? Do
you remember Snake Hosking?' Of course she never met him.
Now I'll have to tell her I spoke with Snake's daughter. There really was a Snake Hosking!"

Identical Dresses Lined Up for the Camera

am intrigued by the pages and pages of my two sisters and me
in my father's album, pose after pose, holding hands, not holding hands, but always right next to each other, sitting as close
as necessary for my father's camera. Maybe I've looked at those
photographs for so long now that I have memorized the clothes
we are wearing, or maybe I actually do remember those clothes:
a checkered dress, brown tie shoes, coats with fake fur around
the collar, corduroy bonnets, zippered overalls, a Davy Crockett
T-shirt, a ruffled sunsuit, three flowered look-alike dresses. Tac-
tile sensations rise out of the photographs: velvet, taffeta, ironed
cotton, itchy sweaters. There is a moment when my seeing and
the memory of cloth come together, and it is as if I've entered the
picture again while the picture comes out to greet me. I am dizzy
and forget where I am, how many miles away from those pictures.

The clothes were passed from sister to sister, so it is difficult to

"Gail, Betty Ann, and Janice outside quarters."

even remember who wore what and when. Like passing a baton, we passed down the clothes my grandmother sent from New Jersey or the clothes my mother bought at the Post Exchange. One by one we took turns growing into something. I am always the tallest in these young photographs, always the skinniest. Betty Ann is the youngest and smallest, always the cutest, so delicious my heart melts now to look at her. Janice is always the middle child, always the roundest, the toughest, later to be better at sports than any of the three of us. We were a package my mother delivered to my father. It was clear that he loved us from the very beginning even though we were not the boys he had planned on.

His camera held us in from infancy on. Here we are on the front steps of our enlisted men's apartment in Fort Bragg, here we are on the front lawn of our tall apartment building in Bad Tölz. A pose by the airstrip, a pose outside a German *Gasthaus*, a picnic pose. The sun is in our eyes, the wind blows our blond hair just a bit to the left. Sometimes there is a grin on our faces, sometimes traces of big tears, but all three of us know already how to pose for my father's camera. Little did we understand then how memory would be contained in those black-and-white images. How some things would never be lost. Little did we know that our father would pass the photographs down, and, sister to sister, we would take turns, like we did wearing the clothes, looking at these pictures over and over again, trying to remember a lifetime far away.

I wanted in those childhood days to get out of that package the three of us formed: the identical dresses, the "Hosking girls." I wanted my own space, dreamed of being an only child, wrote my name on my dolls' foreheads so they wouldn't be mistaken for my sisters'. I wanted to go to the movies without taking them, wanted to go to my friends' without bringing them along. We fought until I sometimes thought I wanted to kill them, as I would often yell out loud. The next rainy day we would create a whole world of a family inside our bedroom with bunk beds. Identical dolls would come out of the closet, each with a similar name, and we would take care of them like they were our own babies. Janice sat in my mother's childhood red rocker and pretended to be the father. I was the mother, and Betty Ann, our child. Scarves and sheets were draped over the bunk bed to create a room within a room, play plastic dishes were brought out of the closet, and boxes were turned over for cradles. It would go on like that for hours until suddenly, for reasons I no longer remember, a fight would break out and someone would yell "MOMMY!" We would separate and go outside to melt into the crowd of other army children, looking for our separate identities.

In the midst of these fights, my mother would often tell us how much she loved her sisters and how someday we would be very happy to have each other. She reminded us constantly what a gift we had and didn't even recognize. I'm not sure any of us ever believed her, couldn't imagine being friends for so many years.

But in the decades since those childhood days, her words have come true. Three separate, three different women have emerged from those times and have sought each other out as if no one else would ever do. Our contact, our separate memories we bring to the visits help cradle the loss that still permeates our lives. It is my sisters I call on the day of my father's death, my sisters who meet me in southern Illinois to arrange our mother's funeral. It is my sisters who recall the front stoops of our many, many apartments; the sounds of our parents yelling in the night; the feel of holding my father's big, broad hand. It is only they who remember my mother's red stretch belt she wore with all her skirts, the ivy she hung on our apartment walls in Germany, the flavor of her banana pudding. They, who wore the same dresses I once wore, remember the sound of my father's stern voice, my mother's cry, the softness of her young skin. They know what it is that will bring me to tears, how my aloofness doesn't mean I don't care. I recognize when their humor is hiding great pain, and I know how to keep their secrets.

February 1955, Dachau, behind the Crematorium

The church I attended as a child of the fortress in Germany, the one that remains the most memorable in my life, was really a chapel, a brand-new stuccolike structure that was small in comparison to churches and synagogues I have visited since. We were living at Flint Kaserne, an American army base surrounded by stone walls that had once been the headquarters of the SS Nazi troops. The Nazis had left no church behind within its walls. But life without a church to most Americans was no life at all, so a chapel was built in the 1950s for the American soldiers and their dependents. The chapel, as we referred to it, housed services for the two religions on base, Catholic and Protestant. In my provincial mind, there were no others. I heard rumors of Presbyterians, Baptists, Methodists, and Mormons, but still you were either a Protestant or a Catholic. The only Jewish presence was in nearby Dachau.

Catholic services were held before Protestant services on Sunday mornings because Protestant children had to go to Sunday school first. The chapel was too small for that, so Sunday school was held in the classrooms above the movie theater. These classrooms were used during the week for soldiers who learned about such things as weapons and war strategies. But on Sunday mornings, one could hear the echoes of patent leather shoes running up and down the wide halls Hitler had left behind, the tune of "Jesus Loves Me, This I Know," and the words of both the Old and New Testaments coming from the mouths of women who spent much time preparing for this weekly hour-long session.

If I managed to run immediately after Sunday school over to the chapel, I would see the priest collecting what my Catholic friends called the "stations of the cross." After he unhooked them one by one off the wall and put them away for the next mass, he would go up to the altar and turn the cross around. I remember that this large brass cross had Jesus hanging on one side but not on the other. Herein, I knew early on, lay the major difference between my Catholic friends' religion and mine. Then the priest would disappear and the Protestant minister would appear as if it had always been just his church.

Something about this chapel and its services drew me most Sundays even if I was the only one in my family to attend. Sunday school was mandatory to my father, but not church. I went anyway. I liked the warmth of the people collected there every Sunday. And I liked the music. I sang in the youth choir wearing a white robe and bellowing out songs whose words still sit just below the surface of my tongue. The choir was directed by a civilian man whose name I've long ago forgotten but whose shy face still comes to me.

He was the music teacher at my school as well. The army hired him to come to Flint Kaserne and teach its dependents. He played the autoharp in school and let us give it a try. We sang American folk songs, Civil War melodies, immigrant songs. It was through these weekly school sing-alongs that I learned about the history and feelings of the American people, of which the songs made me feel a part.

Soon I began attending Wednesday night prayer meetings at the chapel. Not for the prayers, but for the music. Someone would put the page numbers on a board near the altar for songs such as "Onward Christian Soldiers," "For the Beauty of the Earth," or "The Old Rugged Cross," and the group sang like it was starved for the familiar words and melodies. There was always a volunteer to play the piano, which added even more beauty to the songs. When it came time to pray, the prayers were said with as much fervor as the singing. To this day, I remember Alma Elmore's mother prostrate on the floor before the altar praying with her arm around her daughter. It was their genuine humility and radiated love that stay with me. I remember her desperate prayers for her soldier-husband, a nonbeliever, and her prayers for the American home she had left behind.

In civilian life, I never did quite make the leap out of being just a Protestant even though I attended a Baptist church in Illinois and a Presbyterian church in New Jersey and North Carolina. But I could have just as easily been put into a Methodist or Lutheran church, I think. For me, the details never mattered. It was the gathered group itself and the spirit behind the music that drew me in week after week. In the years my father was away in Vietnam, the church became a place to belong, something to ground me when the earth seemed to be spinning off its axis.

In my married life, I converted to Judaism, a shock to many of my Christian friends. But not a surprise when I think about the Old Testament stories I memorized week after week in Sunday school, my love of hearing foreign languages like a chant of ancient music, my search for belonging, and the sense of family Judaism offers. Like the Jews in the Diaspora, I had already acquired a psychological Diaspora from my life as a military brat. I was familiar with alienation from the main group after all my moving from town to town. I was already familiar with Yiddish accents from my life in Germany, I was a puzzle of many homes, and I was content with the melodic sounds of the spirit long before I met a Jew. For me, it was never a giant leap in another direction. Rather, it felt from the beginning as if I were walking along a path and turned ever so slightly to continue my walk; not so much change as destiny.

I recall a photograph my father had my visiting Uncle Bob take of Janice, my parents, and me at the concentration camp at Dachau. I was a five-year-old Protestant then, protected by a skin color, a religion, and a country. I stood with my family in front of a gravestone on which was written "Graves of Thousands Unknown" without any clue that someday my sons, David and Benjamin, would learn the language and ways of the people buried deep within the ground under me. Except for a trick of time, I would have been standing next to their graves, or my own.

I don't remember much from that particular day, but I do remember that my father brought me back to this concentration camp when I was ten years old during our second tour of duty in Germany. He made me look at all the gruesome photographs on the walls, and in somber silence he instilled the horror of the crime done on the ground on which we walked.

Years later I came across this photograph in my father's album and noticed the Star of David in the background for the first time. I realized my father was exposing the child I was then to what can happen to people. Like variations on the myth of Persephone, this warrior father of mine wanted me to know that life was not innocent or guaranteed and could only provisionally be won back. He wanted me to know what he had opposed by fighting in the Second World War. As a soldier he was trying to protect me from such things as Dachau. He was lending credibility to his absences and wanted me to understand that the things he was involved with were big and important and that there were evil things in this world beyond both of our understanding. By bringing me to Dachau, he wanted to fill in the historical gaps of a personal life. I look now with eyes different from those of the five and ten year old I was. I see my father, this teacher of weapons, as both teacher and student of war. He knew that I couldn't possibly understand then but that someday I would.

Italy, 1955

As the summer wind blows back my blond hair, I reach my five-year-old hand up to hold my father's. I smile for his camera, which my mother holds in her hand. My father wears the jacket he wears whenever he's not in uniform, a jacket with his Second World War "509" patch sewn proudly over his heart. With a scowl on his face, he points to the newspaper posted on the cement wall next to us. He is the only one in the photograph who can decipher the words written in bold black letters: "Nesa Della Stampa Communista 1955," meaning "this is of the Communist press, 1955." My father looks like an angry American who has finally found reason to believe the Russians have penetrated the world and that we should not let

Gail by San Marco's Cathedral, Venice, July 1955.

up our vigilance, even while on vacation in a seaport city of
northeastern Italy. He has my mother take a photograph of the
poster in case it could be military evidence. I look carefree in my
sunsuit on this summer day. Communism means nothing to me.
War means nothing to me.

This same month I travel with my parents to Venice, and again
I reach my small hand up to my father's as we climb the stairs at
Saint Mark's Square. Pigeons fly above us as other tourists walk
by. There isn't a cloud in the sky. My father and I are off on an adventure as my mother snaps the picture, which shows our feet
caught in the walking air. This is a moment when father shows
daughter the bigger world, the world of other.

My vision bounces from that quiet photograph to a dream of
destruction where hands and arms and feet no longer belong together. It is my father's death I see in my night's mind, a death too
difficult to comprehend. How to tell a stranger or a blank sheet of

paper hoping for my private words? Even in my dream I keep the details guarded. I dream in a foreign language as if the power of my own might cut through with a knife, leaving more blood like I saw in the destroyed room of my dream. "Destruction, come and see" were the translated German dream words.

My eyes witness, but my heart keeps the knowledge locked up. My pen stops here now, as if to go on is to delve into explanation, into a dark forest of something a girl shouldn't know about. I come to my father's abrupt end, wondering how to do so with a writer's eye. How do I remember the lifetime between our adventures and his death and then make the leap between my childhood and the woman I've become? How do I enter the off-limits zone I learned not to violate as the daughter of a warrior?

Christmas 1956, Wasson, Illinois

Much of the time I worked on this manuscript, I was inclined to leave my mother out of the story. I felt in the beginning that since this was about my father and my search through his photographs, bringing my mother into the narrative would only muddy the picture. It would add another dimension of my father out of the army scene and force me to take the record beyond the photographs, something I wasn't sure I wanted to do.

But eventually I began feeling much like the time the army left my mother off the guest list to the Medal of Honor ceremony at the White House because my parents were officially divorced a week before his death. The army is not one for subtleties. It was as if she was being punished for being a deserter. It didn't matter that she'd been my father's silent partner in the background most of his career. It didn't matter that his orders had been her orders, or that his army life dictated her life. I am reminded in this picture of my mother kissing my father after his return from the Army Language School in Monterey, California, that his life owed a great deal to her life and her waiting for his return.

My mother never saw the Medal of Honor now encased in glass in my uncle's living room. Nor do I remember speaking to her about the White House presentation. I thought at the time that it wasn't right that she wasn't there, but I was a self-absorbed college student then, barely able to keep myself afloat. Those were troubled years, each of us in the family trying his or her best to go on with life, each of us riddled with pain.

The more I worked on this journey to find my father, the more I knew I had to include my mother as well. They met on one of his many roads between wars and lived through his parachute jumps into Greece and Africa, weeks away on maneuvers, letters to Vietnam, and, always, long, lonely nights separated from each other. They had their own private wars as well – struggles with an army dependent's place, alcohol, and the army's demands on our family.

My parents' wedding anniversary, my mother's birthday, the birth of their first child, and eventually my father's death all came in the month of March. Their life together was like that – packed into a small amount of time. Eighteen years rolled by quickly and yet were filled with a lifetime of events: base after base, four children, the cold war, the fear of the Korean War, the endless years of the Vietnam War.

In the end, my mother could not bear up under the strain. Their love, as real as I had witnessed it during my childhood, could not sustain her. The army and war took over. I see in my mind's eye two strangers reaching across the stage, desperate for each other, in love, but, tragically, never able to finally live happily ever after. The curtain closes, and they go their separate ways, still wanting something from each other.

My mother never received any army pay because of my parents' divorce. That in itself helped lead to her downfall. She knew no other way than to live as an army dependent. She had no education, no training. She found jobs here and there as a janitor in an office building after hours or as an aide in a nursing home. There was welfare and money from her children, but nothing enough to truly sustain her without shame. Little by little she gave up.

A neighbor found her dead standing at her kitchen sink, leaning into it on her forearms just as I remember seeing her do so many times when I was growing up. It was as if she was taking a deep breath and wondering just how she was going to get the courage to move on through the day. I sometimes wondered if she wasn't reviewing her whole life in those moments and wondering just how that sweet sixteen-year-old girl who fell in love with a handsome, uniformed soldier ended up in this place.

When the funeral director asked what name we wanted on her gravestone, my sisters and brother and I struggled with a decision. The struggle was in defining who my mother was. "She should be Hosking," my brother said, "because she loved Daddy the most." We all agreed she shouldn't be a Stiff, the man she married soon after my father's death but ended up divorcing as soon as her children could pay for the divorce. The third name she acquired in marriage — to a man we never met and whom she left after one week when she discovered he wouldn't let her sit on his beloved couch — didn't seem like a possibility either.

We chose Gloria Walters, her maiden name, for her gravestone because it was the name she came into this world with. The name and person she was all along. Simple, sweet, and glorious, as her mother often referred to her. In doing so, I feel my sisters and brother and I wanted to relieve her of the men she had stood by and the pain she had suffered. We wanted to cut away the confusion of her life and simply say that here lies Gloria Walters, our mother, the one who gave us life and stood by us for as long as she could before she gave up.

Back at her apartment, we went through her things, trying to decide what to give to strangers and what to keep. We found clothes from another time and another weight, as well as new clothes she hadn't worn yet. Photographs of her children, old birthday cards, and letters from my father were piled together in another dresser drawer. Where were the pearls my father had sent her from Vietnam? Where were her expensive earrings from Europe? Inside her black vinyl purse lying on top of the dresser we found prescription forms not yet filled, pill bottles, chewing gum, notes, more worn old letters. It was the most alive of anything else left in that hot room, looking alert, sleepless, and teeming with mundane existence. We passed her purse around and studied its contents like young children searching for something to play with.

Flint Kaserne

When I first arrived in Bad Tölz, tall pine trees filled the inner square inside the guarded gates of Flint Kaserne. By the second time I lived there, my father said that "some leg" – meaning a soldier who was not airborne – had ordered the trees cut down for a parade ground. I thought about those trees every time I walked over to the library to get more of the orange-covered Famous American biographies I checked out weekly until I had read every single one. I would look out the tall narrow windows from the library's second floor while I sat in a large leather chair and watched uniformed men walk with precision across the parade grounds. My mind wandered to the characters who filled me in those days – pioneers, Revolutionary soldiers, or women like Clara Barton and Dolly Madison. My eyes would travel first out the window to the soldiers below and then to the stacks of books on the wall behind me. The world of the mundane and the imagination bordered each other, and I felt caught between these worlds.

Downstairs below the library was the post theater, which changed its movies daily and charged only fifteen cents for children under twelve. I went to the movies as often as my father would give my sisters and me the money, which he was rarely eager to do. He would make a face as he placed the coins into our hands. We'd run eagerly with friends up the black path, through the gates, and across the parade grounds to the theater before he changed his mind. The library and movies were our classrooms about America. The parade ground with its advancing soldiers seemed in an odd kind of way not to be part of America at all but rather a world in and of itself. I was at home within its guarded gates but at the same time longed to find the world beyond its borders.

My second favorite place on base was the snack bar, where I could buy a popsicle for five cents or a hot fudge sundae for twenty-five cents with my blue, military-issued scrip we used for years instead of American currency. Music, often country and western or Elvis tunes, came out of the juke box. Young soldiers wearing khaki uniforms and smoking cigarettes sat at the tables and chairs. I had been told by someone, I don't remember who now, that we were to ignore those young soldiers as if they weren't there. There was a hint of mistrust which I found unusual since it was the soldiers themselves who created an aura of safety for us in this foreign land. When I left the snack bar, I had to pass the parade ground on a diagonal path. If it happened to be five o'clock, retreat would blow, and all of us — soldiers and children alike — stopped whatever we were doing and stood in silence, hands over our hearts, while the American flag was lowered for the day.

Aunt Lorraine

My maternal grandmother took the name of her oldest daughter, my Aunt Lorraine, from a trucking company because it sounded nice to her. Aunt Lorraine married her a soldier, as my grandmother would say, an Edward Dombrowski who was handsome and suave. It was this uncle who invited my father home for the weekend to meet "one of the sisters." My parents married within weeks of that meeting, and I was born a year after their marriage.

The photograph I find in a packed-away envelope shows the way I remember my aunt the best: sitting in a white sports car parked in the American dependents' housing lot in Munich, Germany, where my Uncle Ed was stationed. She's got her arm up on the seat as she turns toward the camera in a Hollywood kind of swing. If you walked by, you'd get in the driver's seat and take this pretty lady dancing. There's a diamond on her hand and a gold watch around her petite wrist. Her red hair is pulled up in an elegant sweep. She looks as classy as they come. She had that way about her when she'd visit us in Bad Tölz, where we happened to be stationed only an hour away. I thought of them as the rich aunt and uncle because they spent money easily and made life appear so easy.

There was both a friendship and a tension between my father and Uncle Ed, a kind of condescension Uncle Ed brought with him toward my father — nothing I could put my childhood finger on. Once my father telephoned Uncle Ed's apartment in Munich when I was visiting to say he had been picked up for a traffic violation and might have to go to jail. Was there anything Uncle Ed could do to get him out? Uncle Ed laughed in a pure gloating kind of way as if to say, You are the bum, and I'm not. It took me by surprise.

Uncle Ed's job was running the enlisted men's club on base. He would take us there when we visited and let us have all the Coca-Cola, hot sandwiches, and nickels for the juke box we wanted. This was rich living, I thought then. Why didn't my father think so too?

What happened between those rich moments and the next photograph I find is a lifetime, one that runs by you so quickly you can't possibly notice it while it's happening. Uncle Ed was dis-honorably discharged from the army for embezzling funds from the enlisted men's club, and he and Aunt Lorraine divorced. When I was to see Aunt Lorraine again, she was living with her two younger sons in a small two-bedroom apartment in the Harris-burg Housing Project up on Barnett Street. I heard a rumor that Uncle Ed was living up in Chicago somewhere.

Aunt Lorraine's shoulders slope forward in the next photo-graph I find. This one is taken at a picnic under the Eldorado park trees. She puts a Salem cigarette in her mouth. Her lipstick doesn't stay within her lips' lines. Because she's got on a sleeveless blouse, I can tell that her upper arms already look fleshy like my grandmother's. She listens to my teenage sister, whose back faces the camera. There's still a delicate and smooth edge to Aunt Lor-raine's movements – still a part of her that could get into a white sports car and drive away without blinking twice.

In the summer of 1969, I visited her and my mother after my freshman year of college. It had been two years since my father's death and years since Aunt Lorraine had arrived in southern Illi-nois without money in her pocket or a car to drive. My mom and I spent a lot of time in her apartment sipping ice tea out of frosty pink metal glasses. The curtains were always pulled shut but the front door was opened. "Getting any air?" she asked, referring to the fan in the corner. She smoked her cigarettes, and we talked to pass the afternoon. "Get me that hairbrush," she said and then showed me ways to fix my hair. I sat mesmerized by the way she touched my head and the serious way she analyzed my lack of style. Later she turned my hand over, stared down at the engraved skin lines, and tilted her head back while her black, cat-eyed glasses perched on her nose. Rubbing my hands between hers, she said, "You see this life line? It's long, but it's interrupted, like you'll have two different lives. Oh, and see this line? Now that's your head line. Smart girl, am I right, Gloria?" she asked my mother.

In the last photograph I have of Aunt Lorraine, her red hair is unkempt as she sits between her refrigerator and her kitchen dinette set. Yellow-and-green print cafe curtains hang on the window behind the refrigerator. They're too short for the window, so a shade is drawn down underneath them to block out all the backyard light. Aunt Lorraine stares out at the camera like she's not really there at all. It seems like she's living in a world the camera can't reveal, like she's barely aware of us in the same room. Her arm is bent at the elbow and her fingers curl up in a sophisticated stance, reminiscent of her one-time stylish life. An empty Coca-Cola bottle, a jar of instant coffee, a ketchup bottle, and salt and pepper sit on the cluttered table. In a year I would be married and drive through on my way out west with my husband. I don't think I ever saw Aunt Lorraine again after that.

I heard she had cancer and was living in a nursing home outside of Chicago. She died soon afterward in that same nursing home. What had once been part of my self-definition had drifted off with barely a memory intact. What is left is something I feel in my body, a faint sophistication when I suddenly straighten my back and tilt my head sideways. I know it when I look down at my painted nails the way Aunt Lorraine used to do. I remember just then how Aunt Lorraine had once thought of herself as deserving. My body remembers her composure, her confident beauty, the tender way she massaged my shoulders or plotted my life line. I remember the way she could sit still for hours just wondering about the cool breeze coming her way from the small fan in the corner, the way she could size up my face and tell me just what it was I needed.

Group Promotions

My friends at school and in my neighborhood came out of this list: Karen Tally, David Cantu, Mike Lynch, Peggy Joseph. We shared the life of dependents' housing, quartermaster furniture, a once-a-month paycheck with extra treats from the commissary, Thanksgiving dinner at the mess hall, and fathers whose stripes meant everything. We were enlisted men's children, living geographically apart from the officers' children. Our fathers had the same employer and we went to the same schools as the officers' children, but we always knew that when we played with them outside of school, we crossed over invisible lines. We were going against the "Taboo" Mary Edwards Wertsch described in *Military Brats*.

Our world was divided into a system of levels, with the "brass," as my father referred to officers, on one side and the enlisted men on another. There was clearly no social intermingling on the part of our parents. In school I developed antennae for this kind of hierarchy, like having a social mine detector. At home, I was always more comfortable around our side of the base, and I always felt when I walked into an officer's apartment that I probably needed to wipe my feet more.

The thing my father hated more than anything in the army was following the orders of some young lieutenant who knew very little and thought himself to be more important than he was. He would come home and fume with disgust about some "green guy just out of West Point" or joke around calling the soldier names I can no longer remember.

In a photograph taken at the Masons Lodge in Lenggries, Germany, I see my father in a civilian suit standing behind tuxedoed officers — Grand Master Peter Rasmussen to his right, Major Mc-Neil to his left. My father's eyes and closed lips communicate something to me. I remember at once his sense of not belonging, the invisible line he drew between the officers' world and his.

"Rank didn't matter in the Mike Force in Vietnam," one of my father's soldier friends wrote me. "All that mattered was what you knew and what you could do for the team. Your dad knew an incredible amount about survival skills and foreign weapons. He could speak Vietnamese, Cambodian, and French. That's what was important. The hypocrisy of rank disappeared in the jungle."

55 New Street

n the summer of my ninth year, my grandmother came to Europe to visit us. All six of us piled into our blue Opel station wagon, and we took her on a trip through Austria. We picnicked along Lake Constance and saw Lindau Castle before we arrived at the still-bombed-out buildings of Vienna. Driving around the Ringstrasse, we circled the Inner City. I held my grandmother's hand as we walked along the tourist paths, and then I slept in the car leaning my head into her chest.

Most other details of her visit are lost to me, except the one of her sitting in our kitchen on the yellow step stool and crying. I didn't understand then what it was all about. Now I see her visit added a strain where there were already strains: between her and my mother, between her and my father, and between my parents. I see now my grandmother's inclination to pass judgment, my mother's insecurities, my father's struggle to be separate from his mother, and my parents' inability to discuss important things. The discord formed triangles I couldn't break up. I rubbed my grandmother's fleshy arm and hugged her tight.

At the end of my grandmother's visit, my father took her to Bremerhaven, Germany. He stood close to her but not too close, with a stiffness I recognize, as she prepared to board the *Queen Elizabeth*. Her buttoned coat hid her dress underneath but not the dark gloved hand, which clutched a purse. My father smiled, trying to cheer the picture. Sometimes I wonder if my grandmother's sadness that day was about having lost my father already. Did she know somewhere beyond words that my father's life would keep taking him away in bigger concentric circles? Did she know already that he gave her grandchildren who would show love to her in ways he never would?

While my father wandered the globe as a military vagabond, feeling more at home in other lands than in his yellow-and-green childhood house, I learned early on to make myself at home

"November 1959, Bremerhaven, Mom and I."

wherever I was. I learned from the man who never came back to settle on the empty lot next to my grandmother's house not to count on any one place as home, for it can change in an instant with the signing of papers to move on or the pull of adventure. Juxtaposed with this military life was my grandmother, whose living in one place her entire adult life created a stability my family lacked. In my many visits back to her home she taught me that history matters, that the details of one's home make a difference in our lives. She showed me that embroidered pillowcases dried in our own backyard are wonderful to sleep on, and that flowers coming up in the same place year after year reassure us.

My grandmother outlasted my father. At one hundred she still lives in that yellow-and-green house on New Street. Each June I travel there to celebrate her birthday. Her front door opens each time I enter as if we are old friends. Each June I think it's her last. Each time I'm amazed and humbled that I can return. When I do return I feel my stomach quicken, my muscles tighten as though hanging on to something I can't see. I try to act like it's only a visit, only a birthday party, but as I open her drawers and touch books in my grandfather's treasured bookcases, I realize I'm trying to memorize all the details because I feel it's my duty to pass them on. Like a refugee who wants to return to her old house but is unable to find it, I fear one day I will wonder if any of this ever existed.

It's my father's childhood bedroom that fascinates me. I see his furniture left exactly as it was the day he ran away from home, underage, to join the Canadian army and fight in the Second World War. The honey-colored Art Deco bed and matching nightstand face the front windows, and his armoire angles in one corner. It was once filled with my father's uniforms: first the Canadian army, then the United States Coast Guard, and then the Eighty-second Airborne Eisenhower jackets. The quantity of army stuff grew over the years until it ended up in my grandmother's attic and then in my brother's wardrobe. Now only one lone green beret remains in the armoire's drawer.

When I open his closet door, it is not my grandmother's out-of-season clothes I notice but rather the "Miami, Florida" souvenir clothes hook still drilled into the closet's wall that gets my attention. He brought it back after a visit to Aunt Florence one year, my grandmother tells me. Looking at this old remembrance brings me to sudden tears. I see a piece of my father's childhood — for one brief moment a feeling of the actual child who buys a souvenir, believing he will keep it forever. I lean into the closet door as tears pour down my face.

Later I look out his window, now filled with my grandmother's African violets, and see the blue house down the street, the house my sisters and I once called "the Kellys' house." I remember suddenly the photographs of my sisters hanging upside down on the Kellys' swing set. I took those pictures in the days of my first camera, an Agfa given to me by my father when an ocean separated us — his children in his childhood home and he left in the barracks of Flint Kaserne.

The Kelly girls, whose names I'm no longer sure of, ran with my sisters and me through the yards of South Central Avenue and New Street. We became instant friends the year my sisters and I arrived from Germany in the middle of a school year. I taught them a little German: "Der Vater = the father," I wrote on their tiny blackboard in the basement. They tried to teach me French as an exchange, but the German language already took up too much space in my head.

I see now as I look out the window of my father's bedroom that the tennis court at the end of the cul-de-sac is gone and has been replaced by modern homes. It once sat like a private sanctuary surrounded by a wrought-iron fence. Inside that fence as well was a large log cabin, the kind children still build with Lincoln logs. We never knew the owners well, just their daughter, who was ahead of us in school. My sisters and I, along with the Kelly girls, spent hours sneaking over the fence and walking through the bushes looking for secrets at the end of the block.

No matter what room of my grandmother's house I enter now, I hear voices from long-ago Sunday dinners, laughs from her friends playing at a card table set up in the corner, or talk from guests sitting on her couch. I hear my grandmother telling Walter, her widower boyfriend, that dinner is ready. I see him in my mind's eye leaning forward out of the red Queen Anne chair in the corner of the room my grandmother still calls the front room. He shuffles over and sits down at the dining room table, grateful for the meal she places before him. His old black car, older than I had seen before in those days, takes us after dinner up to Franklin Turnpike for ice cream at the Howard Johnson. Later, when I am upstairs with my sisters watching television — *The Mickey Mouse Show*, or *Dragnet*, or *Lassie* — Walter and my grandmother hold hands downstairs in the dark.

I think just then in the middle of that memory that I own so few things that belonged to my parents, but Walter's mother's cordial glasses are in my pantry. My grandmother gave them to me after his death in a nursing home.

Tonight, so many years removed from those times, I sleep with my husband on a pull-out couch in what used to be my Uncle Bob's bedroom but what my grandmother has used now for a long time as a television room. Long gone are my uncle's twin mahogany beds with their carved pineapples on the four posters. Long gone are the stuffed pheasant and stuffed owl my father and uncle shot on their grandfather's farm. Only a few items remain on the walls now; so much has been given away or put into drawers. "Dust catchers," my grandmother says as she waves her hand in disgust.

A photograph of my grandfather, his arms crossed at his chest and a grin forming in the corners of his mouth, stares down at me. Every time I see that picture of him in his tie and white starched shirt, I swear he's smiling at me, proud of his first grandchild, wanting me to know that all these years later.

I learned to iron in this room at the age of thirteen, long after my uncle had left for the navy and marriage to Valentina Kopach. My grandmother sat here with the ironing board set up at the height of her chair and for hours ironed my sisters' and my underwear, pajamas, starched blouses, and pleated skirts. Eventually I practiced myself: collars first, sleeves next, be sure to get the cuffs right, and then the back and sides.

Now I awake in the morning and notice paint coming off the walls. Cracks split like tiny fissures from the bottom of the wall. I imagine my grandmother doesn't notice the dirty smudges anymore left above the heaters. Or if she does, she's resigned herself to life's eventual decay.

All the years my grandmother insisted on dusting every corner and removing every ceiling cobweb in this house are gone now. Even the linen closet's perfectly matched piles are gone. Her curtains used to be washed every spring, and she devoted entire Saturdays to the ritual of cleaning. Gone as well are the years filled with bleach, starch, and fresh sunshine on the clothes pinned on the line outside her kitchen door. "I'm lazy these days," she tells me. "I'd rather sit on the porch."

When 55 New Street is no longer the house of Mrs. Hosking, no longer the same place I recognize in old photographs, no longer the anchor I set down before I leave for other places, I will have lost a piece of visible history. There will be no reference by strangers to my grandmother and the years she coddled this house as if it were life itself.

I want to know, I think to myself as I walk around her rooms, that I carry within me more than enough testimony to the life stemming from my grandmother's house. Somewhere the paths which crossed this part of the world for centuries will show up in the patches of my life's map. Still, the thought of this house passing on to other hands provokes a collection of losses as old as my ancestor Bertholf leaving his family behind in Europe in the 1600s, and as new as my soldier father moving from place to place and finally dying in Vietnam.

Pictures will lead me back to my grandmother's house in my stories and memories. Like a box of mirrors, I want them to reveal every angle, every word that came out of this home. I worry that the bonds of history are not strong enough, not genuine enough, not loud enough to hold the singularity of the lives at 55 New Street. I worry each time I leave her house that ties can be broken forever with the passing of a matriarch. That something much bigger than this house ever was will be lost, and I won't know where to find it.

Maneuvers and War

nce, when I was in fourth grade at the American school in Bad Tölz, Mike Lynch announced in class that my father had been seen running in his underwear through the snowy fields behind the base. I was embarrassed and wondered why my father was there, if in fact it were true at all, because he was supposed to be on maneuvers. For years afterward, I heard this story, usually told with much laughter and beer. During these particular maneuvers, my father was captured and physically restrained in a cell with Sergeant Higgenbotham in Lenggries, miles away from their operating base. The consensus was that anyone captured would be made to talk, and standard procedure dictated moving the operating base if such an event occurred. But the team sergeant knew my father would never divulge the location, so he made the decision to keep the same base. In his cell, my father noticed a tiny window set high in one wall and managed to climb up a pipe and squeeze out. He escaped wearing only his underwear and ran a few kilometers through the snow to quarters on base. Janice remembers being awakened in the early morning hours by my father dressed as a German farmer. He laughed about how he outsmarted the "enemy," then he was gone again.

Thirty-five years later I found Mike's name on an Internet bulletin board. He was looking for men who knew his brother, Jay, who had been killed in Vietnam. I took a chance and sent a message over the Net, not believing I would find a fellow army brat in such a mysterious way. Our messages back and forth relayed descriptions of life at Flint Kaserne, our third-grade teacher, Miss Justine, and mutual friends. I told him how he embarrassed me once with this story about my father on maneuvers. He didn't recall the incident but knew already exactly how my father had been killed. Such news must have traveled far in the Special Forces. Mike told me how his soldier father, who also fought in Vietnam, accompanied Jay's body back to the States. Two telegrams arrived at his mother's house the day Jay died — a mistake made by the army and one that caused her to faint, believing that both her husband and her son had been killed in action. "Get a desk job!" Mike's career-long Special Forces father told Mike before he went to Vietnam. My eyes filled with tears as I read Mike's words written across my computer. I was making a giant leap from third grade to now. I was imagining Mike's mother with that telegram. I was thinking of Mike, Jay, and me once, long ago, safe inside the fortress.

The Collection

The scrapbook I began with my father one afternoon in our Bad Tölz apartment is one of the only items from my childhood that remains. All my dolls, my German leather book bag, and my rock collection are missing; I couldn't trace the threads back to them if I tried. But there in my attic after all the moves, after all the giving things away, is my untouched scrapbook. Its having been packed away and hidden beneath something saved it from destruction. Perhaps it was waiting for me, like my father's photographs, until I was ready to look again. Now that I'm older, the country's older, I am ready to see what it is that was my past, what I can learn from it. I have discovered that giving things away won't erase the past, nor will it protect me from the future.

Each piece of memorabilia was carefully glued in by my father and me, each photograph placed within the black corners he showed me how to use. It occurs to me that he knew that life for a soldier's daughter would be a succession of losses, so he was training me as a collector, showing me how to hang on to things. Objects once of great proportion in a child's life could look to the untrained eye like cheap souvenirs in an aging, water-stained scrapbook, but my father knew, long before I could ever know, that the mundane collected articles would one day tell a story. They are the paths I took with my father in our time together, pieces of who I am.

Now more than three decades later, I turn the pages and find the menu from the Saturday ice-skating matinee at Casa Carioca in Garmisch; Austrian, French, and Spanish money from our summer camping trips; my ticket to Club Carabela, where I watched flamenco dancing one hot summer night in Spain with my father. I am flooded with memories, moments that captured us together. My stamped and certified World Health inoculation record is glued next to a postcard from the International Girl Scout Chalét, where I went with my fellow Scouts. My father wrote "12–14 May 1960" on the postcard's back with his fountain pen. I might have left out this detail, not thinking it would help me one day put my life on the timeline I forgot in the chaos of my family's later years.

On another page I discover a May 1961 Armed Forces Day program with its NATO "Power for Peace" sign written on the front. Scenes of soldiers parachuting out of planes on spring days come back to me, and I recall searching the skies for the one small dot that would be my father and was always beyond my reach. My childhood was filled with these demonstrations of free-fall sky diving, military reviews, and an entire community listening to the American national anthem and standing as straight and tall as anything I've ever seen since. It was packed with words like Colonel Paulick's that day: "All the North Atlantic Treaty Nations agree that constant vigilance is one of the prices of liberty. Through vigilance, surprise attacks on the Free World will be prevented." These were the words that my father's life were caught in, the words that made it all seem so life-and-death serious. I glued them in my scrapbook without knowing I needed to remember, that someday they would be a stepping stone to a life I was desperate to find again — a ticket to a lost world.

I see my 1957 school transfer record stating I was present for forty-one days before I was discharged to another school, another town. The record was glued near a valentine from David Cantu ("David can too, cannot" echoes in my mind from a long ago playground). I recall the endless hellos and good-byes, the chain of new schools until I had collected twelve different ones with twelve new sets of strangers/friends, twelve new sets of teachers. Roxann Castleberry sent me a card from Georgia to Germany, wondering just why I was not writing anymore. I wondered how to hold on to the life I felt was constantly on the edge of loss. How to keep the comings and goings together without the scrapbook?

My father kept track of his friends and his life as well in his photograph albums. Even with his on-the-go life, he made a point to collect and label the photographs of his friends and the places he went. He wrote in that distinctive way he did, always slanting a little to the left, below each photograph or on the back, sometimes in white ink on black pages or black ink on white photograph paper. On one page I see a beach, some distant figures near the Atlantic Ocean, and a young, curly-headed man in just his swimming trunks leaning back onto a railing. My father writes "Tally, Welch Convalescent Hospital, 1945" below the photograph. Later, "Daytona Beach, June 1945, Tally." I see at once he is the man whose name was commonly heard around our Bad Tölz apartment, a man whose army career followed my father's, a man who showed up at my father's funeral as one of the soldiers on funeral detail. My father kept track of Tally's life in his albums, and Tally kept track of my father's body as he flew with it back from Vietnam to New Jersey, where they had first met, which was to be my father's final resting place.

I had kept track of Tally's daughter Karen in my scrapbook for the few years I knew her at the Bad Tölz American school. In one photograph I saved, she stands three girls down from me during a flying up to Girl Scouts ceremony. She was taller than me, blond, with a sweet, boyish face. Neither of us had a uniform like the rest of the girls. Perhaps we hadn't gotten ours in time, but we eventually did and then sewed on each earned badge with great pride just like our fathers had. Years after my father died, I heard that her father had died in a veterans hospital in Washington, D.C. I got Karen's address from Sergeant Higgenbotham, who had visited Tally often when he drove up from North Carolina to Walter Reed Hospital for medical services. It was an awkward letter — what do you say to someone from another lifetime? — and I never heard back from her.

I didn't pursue it because I had already stopped being a collector after my father's death. I got rid of things as if I would never again become attached to anything of value. I was like our country itself, in a haste to leave my past behind. The act of giving away things became a physical act of release. A feeling of safety would overcome me as I drove bags of things to the Goodwill. I believed that sheer owning could choke me of life, and I had to protect myself.

Some days I believe it is a miracle that any of the things from my past survived or that I didn't completely throw away my memory. It surpasses all my understanding that the scrapbook my father began for me and taught me to make could someday lead me, along with my father's photographs, to the lost world I thought I had rid myself of. Surely there was a guardian angel watching over it and protecting it from a final destruction. Along with the rediscovered scrapbook and photographs, I began saving letters from my writing friend, Finvola Drury, because I couldn't bear to throw out the details of our correspondence about my father's life. Nor could I throw out the letters from my father's soldier friends. After years of forgetting my past, I piled these letters on my desk and then in folders, knowing finally that the stories and intuitive understandings were too precious to forget again. I heard my father whisper to me that together we could make room again for the memories.

Two-Man-Carry Rappel

One night during a mountain training exercise in the German Alps, my father fell off a cliff. He had taken a wrong step, but fortunately he only broke a finger in his fall many feet below. Back at the base dispensary, the medics were surprised he wasn't injured more. I remember people saying then how lucky he was — that he had a guardian angel watching over him.

Statistically, my Uncle Bob tells me, my father should have been killed much sooner. It was as if some magic kept him alive through the Second World War, his first tours of duty in Vietnam, many car crashes, and training accidents that killed other soldiers but never him. Statistically, Special Forces soldiers only lasted three months alive in the Mike Force in Vietnam, but my father stayed and kept going back. Then why did he finally get killed, I ask my uncle? Where were his bodyguards? Did he know that he was choosing death when he jumped on the back of the Vietcong prisoner running with a grenade toward the other soldiers? My uncle shrugs his shoulders and reminds me that my father's death wasn't a sneak attack.

I read in Michael Lesy's book *Rescues: The Lives of Heroes* about saving one's self by saving others. I read about the survival of others ensuring the survival of all that was important in the hero. Lesy says that heroism defined as rescue is a conjunction of opposites. To the outsider, heroism is seen as an act of self-sacrifice, but it is also an act of self-reclamation. All the bad a hero knows of himself collides in the conscience with all the good he hopes to be.

I often think of the many opposites of my father: generous but selfish, qualified but disabled, fearless but fearful. I imagine he spent his life wrestling with these opposites. I know now without a doubt, as only those who struggle a long time with a question can come to know, that my father knew what he was doing when he wrapped his arms around the prisoner. I believe he wanted not only to save the Vietnamese and American soldiers in the path of the grenade, but he wanted more than anything to reclaim the self he knew he was losing through divorce and the changes in America. The world he had known was coming apart at the seams.

"You know that line from the Bible?" asks my father's friend Mike McCarthy on the telephone. "The one that says that no greater love hath a man than to lay down his life for his friends? Well, that was your father. It truly was."

Some men are born great, some men achieve greatness, and others have greatness thrust upon them, Lesy quotes William Shakespeare. My father was not born a hero, nor did he achieve in life all that was important to him. He failed by army standards of progressive ranking and by his own standards of creating a family he could return to. But in the end, writes my father's friend Hugh Gordon, "your father died thinking of others. He gave his life so others could live. He knew what he was doing."

Sergeant Higgenbotham, Top Dog

A group of soldiers prepare to get their supplies for a mountain training maneuver in the Alps of southern Germany, one of many maneuvers my father did routinely. They all dress in the same olive drab field uniforms with the same green berets. Ropes that will attach them to each other on their climb hang on their shoulders and touch their waists. In the left-hand corner of the photograph stands a young soldier with a big smile, the buckle of his belt catching the sun. I think I recognize his face the way I think I do so many men in uniform, and yet I must strain to read the name on his fatigues.

Skin color identifies the man behind him as Sergeant Higgenbotham, a friend of my father and a neighbor in our building in Germany. No one called him by his first name. It was always Higgenbotham or Top, meaning Top Dog, because he was one of the first to be promoted to sergeant major at Flint Kaserne. Our families shared occasional meals together in our apartments or on nearby meadows. When my mother felt lonely for her family in America, she cried at their table. When my father damaged his car on an icy German road, it was Higgenbotham he called.

Then we all moved away to new bases. My parents kept in touch with letters, and my father always visited him whenever he came back to Fort Bragg. The next time I remember seeing Higgenbotham was when he drove up from North Carolina to New Jersey with Sergeant Tally in March 1967 on funeral detail. He stood then in my grandmother's house after the funeral dressed in his class A dress uniform in the midst of my white relatives, who passed casseroles around the room. I was too young then, too protective of my own heart to ask about his loss that day, and I wonder now as I write this what it was I would have asked him. How is it one approaches a soldier about war, about losing your friend, about memories?

Twenty-two years later while on vacation in North Carolina, I drove with my husband and children to Fayetteville to visit the Higgenbothams. Tears came to my eyes when I heard his familiar "sweeties" and "yes ma'ams" and his talk about the young Gail he remembered from years past. I realized in that moment that except for some of my relatives, few people know both the girl and the woman. His memories felt like a gift. I didn't have to reinvent for him who I was as a child, the way I've had to do so many times in my life.

We sat at his kitchen table with Betty, his wife, and talked about our years in Europe — how my father would call their home and each time ask, "Is the Sarge in?" We remembered their youngest son, who wore a football helmet in Germany because he kept falling in play, and how ironically he had died in a fall climbing mountains. Higgenbotham talked of parachute jumps into drop zones, maneuvers code-named things like "Operation Devil's Strike," and his memories of the now legendary maneuver story of him and my father imprisoned together in a cell in Leng-gries where my father got out. "That guard never could figure out what happened to the other prisoner!" Higgenbotham said.

Then he showed me a photograph of John F. Kennedy viewing the Tenth Special Forces in Berlin in 1961 and asked me if I remembered that happening. There in the first row, looking young, strong, and quite proud, sat Sergeant Higgenbotham holding the American flag — noticeably the only black soldier in the group. I asked him about this, and his stories led to the Triple Nickels, an all-black unit he fought with in Korea. He spoke then about growing up in Harlem — how once, after finishing his first stint in the army, he returned home, only to see his school buddies job-less, standing on street corners, asking him for money: "Hey Hig! You got a ten?" Within forty-eight hours, he flew back to the base and reenlisted for life.

"Yes ma'am. This army stuff gets in your blood," he said, com-menting on his career in the army. "I like the comradeship — we're all in the same boat together in the army. What we do is helpful for all. Soon you get divorced from civilian life, and the army becomes your world." Old soldiers stay soldiers forever, to paraphrase the old saying. Like in this photograph, there is a rope that holds soldiers together, keeps them depending on each other. The army has a way of turning strangers into family.

I heard from Betty years later that Higgenbotham died. What he thought had been back pain from his years of parachute jump-ing turned out to be bone cancer, finally diagnosed by his doctor daughter Gwen. Betty says it was caused from his time in Utah when the army stationed soldiers near atomic experiments. She was to find out that Higgenbotham was the last of those men to die, the rest having died from cancer much earlier. Betty said that he had written her during that Utah stay about the rabbits without hair and the eerie feel of the air. "Why did he go, then?" I asked her over the phone.

"You know soldiers, Gail. You go because you're told."

Pallbearers came from the 555th Parachute Infantry (the Triple Nickels), the Rangers Infantry Company Airborne of the Korean War, and the Special Forces. They filled the church that day and carried a man who came out of Harlem to become the kind of soldier my father always admired — the kind who refused to be just an ordinary GI on the streets.

In Disguise

he black car door in this photograph opens, and out steps my father dressed in a German hunter's outfit. The only thing that gives away the place is the license plate, which begins with the letters TÖL, signifying Bad Tölz. Perhaps my father is on maneuvers and slipping in and out of the German countryside, hiding from the pretend "enemy." If that's the case, he's doing a good job, because it's difficult to tell he's an American. If I didn't know his face, I would think him to be a Bavarian hunter.

I'd like to say my father was a man of disguises, but I didn't know it then. I only know that now, looking back, seeing him move in and out of places with complete ease. When he spoke Czech with a perfect accent to our housecleaner and friend, Maria Joachimstahler, and then switched to English when he spoke to me, or German to the local beer deliverer, it was as if I was witnessing separate people within my father, each with their own language. Another minute he polished my shoes for school and then was off drinking with buddies or disappearing, only to show up in a land called Vietnam. He laughed and talked about the Vietnamese soldiers cutting off the ears of prisoners, and I buried this knowledge.

Even my father's age is in disguise. His face looks ageless to me in his photographs. Twenty-five, thirty-five, forty-two — it all looks

Ein deutscher Jäger.

the same on him. Whatever it was that advanced his years does not show up in a photograph. It is yet another mask.

I search for his face when I look through books about Vietnam. I cannot resist looking for the shelf of related books and turning the pages, hoping he'll show up there. But the pages begin to blur, and there are suddenly no individual faces. It's as if they all cloud together, wearing masks I can't see through. My father is lost in the crowd, obscured with sheer numbers of the dead.

In a scene described by Tom Corbett, I see my father during one Christmas week in the mess hall on Fort Bragg's Smoke Bomb Hill. My father told him he would soon be returning to Vietnam, and he was both looking forward to it and resenting it, as it meant a year of family separation. He said he loved the army and the Special Forces, but he also loved his family very much. He had quite separate roles, and it was often too difficult to play both at the same time.

Memory's Pull

The blue of the Mediterranean Sea rolls into the sloping coastline north of Barcelona, Spain. It hits the large rocks, leaves its memory, and sweeps back out, only to roll in again.

In the foreground, on a dusty dry hill, my sisters and I pose with my father during our summer vacation. The hot sun shines off his gold watch and wedding ring onto the turquoise tattoo on his forearm. Betty Ann moves in and puts her arm around Janice's back, feeling her long braids. We are all touching — shoulder to shoulder — and then the camera clicks and the moment is framed, forever unyielding.

The pain on my shoulders returns, and I know again why I am wearing my blue shirt backwards. The blisters of yesterday's strong sun remain, and it is the collar turned the right way that rubs. I fiddle with wooden painted castanets as the sea breezes blow by the camera. The warmth of the Spanish sun rises through my sandals from the dry earth below me. I reach behind and feel the blond hair on my father's arms. I see the hollowed-out part of his thigh from a bazooka accident years before, the skin tight and scarred. It is something he can never disguise. I hear his familiar voice and know we all belong to each other. I feel his bristly face as it rubs with a kiss against mine. I touch his shoulders, feel his strong muscles, and remember his lifting me up. It is all there

July 1961, Spain.

suddenly, as though it never left. And then the sea rolls out again, and the memory pulls away.

July 1961, Bad Tölz

My father awkwardly holds my infant brother, Wesley, the son he said he always wanted, a boy after several miscarriages and three daughters. Ironically, with the joy of my brother's birth came the downfall of a long marriage. Fourteen months later, on a cold winter day, we left my father standing at the port of Bremerhaven while we returned to the United States. My memory snowballs here from bad to worse, and I am left with only glimpses of time. There were moves between grandparents and then a reconciliation as we tried again to live together in North Carolina. The memory revives, and I see my father leaving for Vietnam. We never lived together for more than a few months after that.

In the end, my siblings and I went to live with my Uncle Bob and Aunt Val. My brother at the age of six became my uncle's only son. He has no recollection of my father. This photograph and their being together doesn't exist for him. It is my uncle who is "Dad," not this man he grew up to look like.

I hear my brother's voice on the phone and my father's voice trails closely behind. His laugh sparks a partial memory, and I'm at once with my sisters riding on my father's back, giggling as we fall off. I see my brother reading with an earnest look on his face, and I know I have seen this movie before. Only there aren't any reruns to show my brother. The past is wiped out for him as though it never happened.

My mother's shadow appears in the right-hand corner of this photograph because she faced the sun when she took the picture. More like a photograph of shadows than of real people, the edges of my father and brother are unclear in the sun in which they fade.

When Wesley was six years old, a soldier handed him a flag at my father's funeral. At the same moment, he heard guns go off in a salute behind him. I remember him smiling real big the way he did so well in those days and standing at attention like the play soldier he was. But he wasn't wearing the jungle hat and fatigues my father had a Vietnamese tailor size for him — the uniform he wore most days while my father was gone. He was dressed instead in a sports coat which he had never worn before and something that just didn't look like him. I think he thought the flag was a gift for being a good boy or a toy he might play with when the party was over. He had no idea what it really meant when they lowered my father's casket into the grave. It had been months since he had seen my father, and even then he saw him for only a short time before my father returned again to Vietnam. I remember he called my father his "soldier daddy," as if he had more than one and as if this daddy could only be described that way.

My brother was a sickly child from the beginning of his life. He was born with a hole in his heart, and my parents were told he'd never play sports. Later, he developed a perforated femur and spent over a year in a body cast. Then there was "water on the knee," the doctors called it, and an awkward gait. Later, asthma pulled on his every breath for weeks at a time. Through it all, he was a happy boy, prone to big smiles and cheerfulness. I know Wesley's illnesses saddened my father because he always mentioned him in his letters, asking us to take extra care of him. Eventually good health came to my brother after a long list of ailments. One wouldn't know now to look at him that such things had ever occurred.

What none of us can see are the scars a six-year-old boy gets when he looks up to tall uniformed men and holds out his small arms for a folded flag. That image of the Hero becomes a part of that little boy in ways none of us can measure. It has to find its place somewhere buried in who the boy becomes later. His father finished something he could never do. I sometimes wonder if that's why my brother begins so many things and finds it difficult to finish them. The world has asked of my brother what he can never be — it has asked him to be the son of my father, the Hero, and to find a place for that inside the man he's become, a near impossible task. He must live with the figurative presence of my father in his lifetime and in this country, but never with the actual man.

Lilian, a first cousin of my father, sent my brother a bedspread on which she had sewn all my father's army patches. The patches were all colors: a white airplane with a white parachute behind it on a blue background, gold lightning bolts over a gold sword, black lightning bolts over a black sword on an olive-drab background, a blue dragon on a white background, and on and on. There were letters like "AA," and numbers like "101st" and "509." They meant nothing to my brother, except they meant everything. Here was his soldier daddy's life covering him in the safety of his new father's home.

When he was a teenager, he said he wanted to join the army, but my uncle discouraged him. I don't remember why, but I think it must have had something to do with his only brother's death, how he couldn't have sustained one more loss in his life. Perhaps my uncle knew that the son of my father, who became the son of my uncle, could never be my father, and that life in the army might demand that of him in one way or another. My uncle grew to love my brother like a son, and my brother grew to love my uncle as a father. My brother has called my Uncle Bob "Dad" since he was six years old. My uncle has called my brother "Son" since the day we moved in with him and Aunt Val. Neither my uncle nor my brother chose each other, and yet they created from scratch something my brother never had with his soldier daddy.

Several times after college my brother got close to signing up for the army. He talked about it for weeks ahead of time as if he were expecting us to argue with him and talk him out of it. In the end he said it was my Uncle Bob's talking him out of it that kept him from doing what he "really wanted to do." I suspect he needed to join and he needed not to join. Perhaps there was the hope of following in my father's footsteps and the real fear that no one ever could. Eventually, he passed the age where the military would accept him, and we never talked about it again.

October 1961, Champs-Elysées

The only information I have about this photograph lies in this title, written by my father on the back. I have no idea why my father is here or whose shadowy form with camera in hand appears at the bottom. I can only guess my father will visit the nearby Arc de Triomphe, an impressive monument honoring Napoleon I's military victories, and the Place de la Concorde, where people were once executed during the French Revolution. He must have known that the French were still involved in war, this time in Southeast Asia. What he doesn't know this fall morning is that American soldiers will take over the fighting. The French will leave, and my father will find himself swimming in the abandoned French Club pool near his camp at Loc Ninh, Vietnam. The view from the dressing cabana will be of palm trees and rolling hills. It will be so calm it will even fool my father's camera.

Robert Simmons, once a roommate of my father, told me about a cache up in the Alps where my father hid C rations, a pair of boots, a change of clothes, matches — all in case of war. "We were on alert at all times in those days in Europe," he said. "We knew in case of another war we would be the first target for the Soviets. Each time the alert sounded we didn't know if it was real or not. We were only told to bring gear to a certain location or to be ready to parachute into an area. We had no idea where we were going, only that we must be ready to fight. Sometimes we didn't come home at night because of a surprise alert. We could be gone for three to five days, or sometimes three to five weeks. Our wives had no idea when we'd return. Some soldier had the job of going around to the wives and giving them the keys to their cars and telling them it was an alert. We were always ready for war. Your father was more prepared than the rest of us with his cache in the mountains."

I wonder if my father left his cache in the Alps, believing war was imminent with the Soviet Union, or if he took those things and buried them somewhere in the jungles of Vietnam. What he couldn't have known in the fall of 1961 when he visited Paris was that there are some things we can never prepare for. Some things we can never retrieve once they're lost to us.

December 1963, on the Way to Vietnam

Postcards from Travis Air Force Base and Wake Island, places my father stopped at before arriving in Vietnam, must have come to our North Carolina home, but I don't recollect what they looked like. I remember instead my friends Terry and Pat, North Carolina history, and notes from my young home economics teacher about how to can vegetables. I remember thinking that the southern civilian method of putting whites in one school and blacks in another didn't make any sense to me. I was long accustomed to integration in the army and having friends like the Higgenbothams and Arlene Jackson.

I probably wrote my father, but not nearly enough letters. I never told him about the social dancing lessons I had taken that spring while in New Jersey, nor did I tell him or deem it possible to say that my menstrual cycle had begun in his absence. I didn't mention how lonely I felt or how different life was outside the fortress – that it was like living in no-man's-land, neither here nor there.

Sgt. Frank Badaloti, a young Special Forces friend of my father, sent my sisters and me black lacquered jewelry boxes from Vietnam. He was the first person we knew to go there. He wrote us letters the way a pen pal might, and we enjoyed his attention. When this New Hampshire man was killed, we were stunned and unable to fathom the turn of events. Perhaps in not writing my father very often after that I was already preparing for our final separation. The world of safety had a crack in it, and we all knew it suddenly without saying a word.

"Guarding Agency Plane with Special Platoon, Loc Ninh."

On Guard

I gather from a Philippine postcard my father sent my mother that he arrived in Vietnam for the first time in the middle of December 1963. "Will write after I arrive at destination," he scribbled from Clark Air Force Base. Always in military code — no more details than that. Before my father knew it, it was 1964 and he was guarding a small airplane parked alongside a fence at the Loc Ninh airfield. Eight well-armed soldiers, members of a squad from the Special Platoon of Cambodians and Chinese mercenaries he trained, stood around the plane my father called an "agency plane" on the back of the photograph.

General Westmoreland, who had come to check on my father after his Fort Campbell training accident years before, visited Loc Ninh in 1964. Perhaps he flew in on one of the planes my father guarded. Maybe he even remembered my father from that day back in 1951. Maybe not. After he inspected the troops, shared some words, and spent some time boosting morale, he left. Unlike Agamemnon, Westmoreland did not share every soldier's risk on the battlefield. The price of trying to organize the world for liberty as he and John F. Kennedy believed cost our country more than anyone had bargained for. By the end of 1964, there were 23,300 U.S. servicemen in the Republic of Vietnam, my father among them. The seduction of power and the complicated politics of nations continued their pull on this country. But to the men in this photograph, the focus was far more simple: this plane, this operation, these soldiers.

My father spoke highly of the Cambodian soldiers he trained. They were a dignified people, honest, trustworthy, and loyal, he once told me on one of his visits home. Roy Matthews wrote me that my father feared early on that when the Vietnam War was over, it would continue into Cambodia, and if it did, he said he would return to fight for them. My father was right, history tells me, and what happened to the Cambodian people with Pol Pot's killing fields defies my imagination. I believe my father's spirit was in Cambodia witnessing this massacre and weeping for those to whom he had entrusted his life. I imagine that his rage at what the higher-ups ignored and must have known all along still haunts his restless spirit.

Loc Ninh Photographic Collage, 1964

found Loc Ninh on the map. It's in the Third Corps, one of the four areas into which South Vietnam had been militarily divided by the United States. Its district headquarters is near the Cambodian border and on the same highway that leads to An Loc and eventually Saigon. Camp Loc Ninh is home to my father and the civilian irregular defense groups that he trains. Judging from the photographs I see in his album, an armed soldier stands at the guard post as you drive up to the camp. Once you get by him and inside the camp, you see some soldiers working on a hoist for vehicle repair and some others loading up an open truck headed for an operation outside the camp. Walking farther, you see sandbags surrounding the communications bunker and the ammo storage under cover. A switchboard inside operates the claymore mines electrically. My father's AR-15 rifle leans against the sandbags inside this mortar bunker, while a lone snake squirms on the dry dirt.

Outside the bunker, some Strike Force soldiers play basketball near a wall of sandbags. Farther inside, you might run into

Jim Keene, Captain Hubbard, Lieutenant Evetts, and Lindewold (MIA). My father and Sergeant Silvernail barbecue steaks on a makeshift grill. They are outside a thatched hut with walls woven in a zigzag pattern. Silvernail is in his underwear, and my father doesn't wear a shirt. His dog tags touch his chest. His eyes squint and his face grimaces from the smoke as he reaches over to cover a pot on the grill.

Kim San, the Special Force's company commander's bodyguard, squats on the ground nearby while he compares a U.S. M-26 hand grenade with a VC (Chinese made) one. He wonders which one works better. Tan, the Vietnamese interpreter, and Toc Don, the Cambodian interpreter, must be around somewhere. So is Toc Lan, the commanding officer of Company 309.

I can see from my father's photographs the strands of places he was and the people he knew. I weave them together like the straw hats of the Vietnamese peasants. What is always left out no matter how hard I try or how closely I look are the sounds he heard. I can't hear the sounds of death. Sometimes I feel as if the photographs disguise why he was really there, what it was that he carried with him from place to place in Vietnam and then back home for a while. In that way the photographs themselves become a mask. The pictures were there from the beginning, but not so the sounds he couldn't translate for me.

Another Hitch

My father snapped a picture of the military transport plane he took on his way home from his first tour of duty in the Republic of South Vietnam. He stopped at Clark Airfield in the Philippines and then in Japan and Alaska before he arrived home. He left war one minute and the next minute sat in an air-conditioned plane with a beautiful hostess bringing him a tray of American food. Turn off one world. Turn on the next.

How did my father think he'd find us? Did he think he'd enter our lives as though we'd stood still waiting for his return? He came home too late to watch me graduate from junior high school

"Discharge and Reenlistment, December 1964."

wearing the first dress I ever made, and he didn't know I had had my first kiss. I don't even know if he ever knew how much I needed him.

The same month my father returned from Vietnam, he stood under a large oil painting of John F. Kennedy and shook the hand of Gen. William B. Yarborough, who like my father had fought in the 509th Paratroopers during the Second World War. While someone photographed the moment, the general handed my father an official certificate acknowledging my father's signing on for yet another hitch in the army. It wasn't the first time he had reenlisted.

My father talked at times about getting out of the army. He dreamed of teaching at West Point. I don't know if he said this to appease my mother or if he really thought he could leave the army. After many years of moving his family in the military routine, he sometimes thought that civilian life in the States might not be so bad. But each time he came close to a discharge he reenlisted, and the life began again.

The army had become home. My father deceived himself that he could leave the familiar atmosphere where someone else is always in charge of you and you are responsible for your one assignment. It was said by Yoram Kaniuk, the Israeli author, that the army is the closest thing to God. Or at least the Catholic Church, which recognizes that you can't find free will in paradise, the army, or the church but that you can find happiness and peace of mind under the command of an omniscient power.

Attack on a Village, Phuoc Long Province, March 1965

My father arrived this month in Vietnam for his second tour of duty. He left me and my sisters at my grandmother's, in the house where he was born. While I turned fifteen, I attended his old high school and sang in the choir at his childhood Presbyterian church. I can't retrieve the memory of that birthday, nor can I remember for the life of me how I felt about my father then. It's buried somewhere in layers of defense, hidden in the months I chose not to examine anything. I kept a cheerful face with Girl Scouts, friends, and school, pretending to the world and myself, particularly myself, how absolutely normal everything was. The subject of war or being a soldier's daughter never came up. I just put my feet in the motions of forward movement and listened intensely to music.

In this photograph of my father at war — not resting, eating, or preparing but actually in the action of war — I am surprised at his smile. I am told by my father's friend Harry McGloughlin that if a soldier allows his sensitivity to sit within himself, it will be his sure ticket to death. A soldier must have an adrenaline edge in order to protect and be protected. Otherwise he stands defenseless, he said. It's as if a soldier must have a continuous split personality. I wonder what it is about the army that supplies men and their daughters with a way to separate the senses.

I ask my father's soldier friends why my father went to Vietnam three times. How could he keep leaving his family? They write me that my father loved his family very much but that it was his belief that until the job was finished, he had to be there. As long as there was one American there, he felt it was his duty to be there as well. My father's soldier friends write me that my father fought for his family, his comrades, his country, and his mission — in that order.

I can't comprehend or believe that my father fought for my family in any specific sense. It was bigger than that, I think, for him. He was pulled like a magnet toward his job as if his legs already knew how to make gigantic leaps across oceans to strange lands, as if his hands always knew the feel of weapons, his ears the sounds of war. Buried within that forceful tug was his hope that what he did would affect his family positively in the long run. In the narrow corridors of jungle life, I believe his comrades and mission filled his mind, while country and family faded into the distance of what used to be home.

July 13, 1965, Escape from the Vietcong

Isaac Camacho was the first American to escape from the Vietcong. He stood between my father and Rocky Lane in this photograph taken at the outpost of Company C, Fifth Special Forces. I found out almost three decades later in a letter from him that after he found his way through the jungle, it was my father who ran around getting him boots and a new uniform and trying to feed him all the food he could consume. Camacho wrote me that he was forever grateful for my father's attentiveness that day. He remembered also the way my father told stories that kept the other soldiers laughing. He enjoyed the way my father paid attention to details.

After a shower and a meal, the camera caught Camacho talking to the men around him, one of them my father, who looked at the camera as if he was guarding the area. Camacho was the only one smiling. I imagine he hasn't felt this kind of comfort since before his captivity. I wonder what he did with the imprisoned years of his life that can't be explained to anyone. How did he find his way back to my father's outpost on unfamiliar jungle trails? What were his ways to defeat devastation and horror? Where do his ghosts reside?

The dictionary says that courage is the quality of mind that enables one to encounter danger without fear. As Tim O'Brien writes in his novel *Going after Cacciato*, courage can't be about fear or no fear. It's got to be about acting wisely in spite of the dread. Or maybe, as O'Brien says, it's about finding within ourselves a lone chromosome that when made to fire can produce valor.

I wonder if there is such a gene inside me. My writing friend tells me I will isolate the lone chromosome in writing. That is where I will find my determination and spirit.

A Near Miss

When my Uncle Bob was a sales executive for CBS Radio in New York, he was called into his boss's office one day before lunch. The boss informed him that news had come over the wire service which indicated a heavy attack on my father's camp in Vietnam. A couple of hours later, my uncle was called back and told this time that the enemy had broken through the camp walls and later that the camp had been overrun completely.

While waiting for a confirmation from the State Department, Uncle Bob worried how he would break the news to his mother. The next day, before any phone calls, a letter arrived from my father saying that he was recovering in a hospital in Saigon. He had fallen from a footbridge the day before the attack and had broken his ankle. The army had flown him out of the camp by helicopter.

August 1965, Ten-Minute Break

What these soldiers resting in a rubber tree grove in Vietnam accomplished on their mission is not written on the back of this photograph. Nor is there evidence on the front. My father, the only one standing, looks as though he hasn't slept for days. His eyes appear to droop in the heat of the midday air. The dictionary defines rest as freedom from toil and strain. Yet the exertion of the mission remains on the soldiers' shadowed faces during this ten-minute break. They appear to know, as Shakespeare wrote in *Julius Caesar*, that "death, a necessary end, will come when it will come."

In August 1965, on the other side of the globe, I thought that no one except soldiers knew about Vietnam. I knew it was mentioned on television, but only as a small part of world news, not because it was a big deal. I convinced myself it was maneuvers, a practice of war, another assignment from which my father would return, and we would then get orders to a new place. I remember someone in the small town in Illinois where I lived asking me where my father was. I replied that he was assigned to a place she had probably never heard of: Vietnam. I look back now and know it was a defense — that kind of magical thinking children do, believing in their own powers to create the world's reality. I had fallen silent just like many of the returning soldiers. Like them, I couldn't use real war language like "legs blown off, bled to death, crying all night," even if I could have known such descriptions then. I chose instead the world of ignorance and invisibility.

It is only now, years away from this war, that I can listen to the soldiers' voices as well as the voices from those involved in the peace movement. In the years my father was at war and in the years following his death, I couldn't listen to either. I was caught in no-man's-land. It seemed to me then — if I ever consciously thought about it, and I didn't do much of that — that these were clearly labeled sides, and neither could define where I was. There was a vague sense that if I marched against the war, I was marching against my father. And if I really believed in the war and thought everyone should fight it, I was marching against a truth I didn't believe in. From the periphery I watched some of my college peers' hatred for the war get caught up in hatred for the soldier: attempts to burn down ROTC buildings, the inability to speak again to those who were drafted, making fun of military uniforms. Only now can I see that it was a mere assigning of blame, like a child's desperate need not to censure a parent (our country). I often felt like a stranger among my peers, but neither would I have felt at home within the fortress. I built a wall inside myself instead.

All these years later I can also pay attention to the experience people like my friend Finvola had at that time. She, along with many, worked with mothers, fathers, priests, rabbis, teachers, and writers who fought our government's decision to send in thousands of troops for years and years to a place even the soldiers were saying we didn't belong. They wanted the killing stopped,

Looking toward north end of Camp Minh Thanh, RVN.

wanted the sight of fresh graves and grieving parents to end. Many in this movement fought through rude, humiliating encounters with senators and congressmen, all for the sake of bringing humanity back to our country.

It seems to me that our country has not rested from Vietnam. The wounds still bleed when pricked. A graduate school colleague reads a piece she wrote about her fiancé's death in Vietnam, and there is a familiar hush in the audience. I look around and see tears from seemingly strong and unaffected people. Soldiers I don't know and long-time friends record the faith they have lost in our leaders. Pictures of young men just out of high school who never returned from the war still sit on tables in many homes. A song from that era comes out of the radio, and I swear I can see the memories still written across our faces.

Dream

am walking down the streets of Saigon with my three-year-old son. We find a playground and see my soldier father there. He is without his shirt, and his tiger-striped pants are tucked into very dusty jungle boots. I recognize for the first time his fatigue from the war: the sweat, heat, and pure loneliness. Near a large

rusted garbage container, I suddenly see a long black serpent com-
ing toward me. It is ugly beyond words, and it moves like an inch-
worm, the back part moving slowly to reach the front. It won't let
me alone. I am frightened of this snake my father calls a bonger.
"Where's my pistol?" my father asks. He says it's the only way to
get rid of bongers, unfortunately. He's sorry to have to do it, but he
must. Before he's finished, he has killed three bongers.

Instructing at the Sand Table, Camp Minh Thanh

My father has the full attention of five ARVN (Army of the Republic of Vietnam) soldiers in this photograph as he leans over an instructional sand table. He is their teacher, the one who informs them of military strategies in their country. It is my father who speaks to them in their language; it is he who has traveled away from his own people to live with them.

I think back to the summer of 1965 and see that I was teaching strangers how big my smile could be. I taught them that war didn't affect families and that daughters could be safe without fathers. I tried to teach my sisters that if we ignored the obvious empty chair at the table, by magic it wouldn't affect us. Like my father's self-assured hands in this photograph, I conveyed my teachings in silence.

Now every time I see a Vietnamese man I wonder if he knew my father. Might he have been one of my father's bodyguards? I wonder about that kind of loyalty, that intimate regard that allows one to risk one's life for another.

I wonder as well if he might be one of the hundreds of NVA (North Vietnamese Army) soldiers who defected from the north through the "Chieu Hoi" program and, with a simple rifle and a paycheck, switched sides. I am told they became the so-called Kit Carson scouts for the American army. I can only imagine that after the war they suffered greatly for their defection. It makes me wonder about our leaders, who never considered such people in their decision to quickly escape Vietnam and who left whole fields of jeeps, tanks, and broken lives behind.

My father's life merged with the Vietnamese and Cambodian culture during his time at war. Each tour of duty yielded another new layer. It wasn't just the war that changed him but the people themselves who did. Even on his return visits home, I could see the impact on him — the way he dressed in Vietnamese black clothes, the rice he ate sitting cross-legged on the floor, his insistence that his daughters wear Buddha necklaces for protection, and the positive way he spoke about the soldiers he trained.

In my father's final act, his body merged physically with the body of a stranger, so much so that it was difficult, I've been told, to know where his life began and the stranger's ended. What was left on the ground that day is beyond a daughter's imagination. I can only see it as a symbolic merging — the known with the unknown and the American with the Vietnamese culture.

On the back of one photograph taken in Binh Duong Province, my father wrote: "Russian Model 1944 carbine carried by VC I killed on operation near Saigon River." At first all I can imagine is his documenting proof that the Russians were indeed involved, as they had been during so many of his war years. Then suddenly I imagine my father's rifle and rucksack contents lined up for view by the North Vietnamese. How absolutely lonely my mind's photograph remains.

The writer, Bao Ninh, who fought in the war as a North Vietnamese soldier, writes about war's naked face. He is of my generation, born only two years after me. His life now in middle age has a dominant sense of loss and disillusionment, much like many soldiers here have. In his novel *The Sorrow of War* he asks, "When will my heart be free of the tight grip of war?" I have asked myself, the nonsoldier, the same thing. "My soul is still in turmoil," he writes. "The past years imprison me. It is the generals who like to talk about victory and defeats, but the common soldier doesn't speak of such things. Writing is my last duty as a soldier."

After my father's second tour of duty, my uncle asked him what it would take to win the war. "It will take a standing army of a million," he said, "and the minute we leave it will go back the way it was before we got there." This soldier father of mine, the one who gave both countries all he had to give, was right. Death in-

"Minh Thanh, August 1965, Rocky Lane."

truded on his life. Now obligation intrudes on my solitude, just like it does Bao Ninh. Writing about my father and the war is my last duty as a daughter.

Questions

Rocky Lane and my father sit on top of a dusty jeep, their feet dangling, making it unclear whose foot is attached to which leg. Except for the undershirt showing underneath his fatigues, Rocky Lane's uniform is exactly like my father's. Even the tattoos and watches look alike. The background of rubber trees, dry leaves, and radiating sunshine seems to grow brighter and larger with each minute I stare at this photograph as if, like one large fire, it could spread and melt whatever I remember about my father. His quiet grin and relaxed look con-

"August 1965, Minh Thanh, Demo Training."

trast with my views of war and the loud beats I feel pounding in my chest.

There's not much else to speak about in this photograph. Just some soldiers under the shade of silver trees, smiling into the camera, their wool berets covering their short haircuts. Soldiers at rest in the middle of somewhere. No weapons around. No fear on any face. No surprises. No questions. Well, maybe one: why is Rocky Lane wearing his wedding ring and my father isn't?

Training

While my father trained Cambodians near the rubber plantation of Minh Thanh, I moved from my grandmother's house in New Jersey to my mother's alley apartment in Harrisburg, Illinois. While his jungle boots, like laced-up canvas sneakers, got soaked with blood and rain, I ordered a blue blouse out of the Sears catalog. While the sun bleached out his blond hair, I let my schoolgirl hair grow long. While his cheek wound healed, I watched my mother lock horns with loneliness. While my father trained soldiers he could count on in the jungle, we learned not to count on him.

Underneath the Map – Rooms of War
and Perpetual Dusk

You ask me about the places, the dates, and I try hard to remember. I lived here, and then I lived there – North Carolina, Kentucky, southern Illinois. Or was it New Jersey? The army base in Germany? In between I mention the Vietnam War, when my father left to fight, the outhouse at Momo's. I tell you that's Appalachian mountain talk for grandma, and you just keep listening like you're waiting for a punch line, like you couldn't bear to hear one more word about Vietnam.

What I give you is a chain of events neatly connected together, but it's not how it really was. I paint only the surface, like a bird's view of the earth it flies over. My memory can't be followed like a map.

How it really happened shows up in the visual details that flash underneath the map over and over again – the ones that wake me in the middle of the night to see rooms as if they're on permanent display.

One room appeared the other night in a dream with no plot. The lights came on in the dream's corner, but the light wouldn't reveal everything because it was covered with a scarf. My mother used to do that. I know only now that she wanted to leave the room's details up to her imagination. She wanted to pretend that her couches weren't worn, that rugs weren't dirty. She wanted to sit in those rooms and take some deep breaths after we'd gone to sleep. It became her place of waiting for my father to return from war like a knight in shining armor. I imagine her vision of him saluting the flag and rushing to hug her, promising this time that everything was going to be all right.

Telling when he left and when he returned and where we moved next is the time line I present. But what does that tell of waiting in dimly lit rooms or of my mother's tears which I never connected to her life? What did I know then of love? What did I know of waiting for the father of your children?

I knew only of those rooms. Always we picked up like immigrants and moved to a new base, a new town, a new apartment. As a child I used to draw maps of rooms detailed with where the furniture sat and how the curtains draped back. In third grade, my blond, pony-tailed teacher asked us to draw a map of our apartment, and I made it look different from all the other army dependents' apartments. I knew my drawing was a lie, but even my conscience didn't prevent me from imagining.

One room, a place of giggling as my sisters and I fell off my father's pretend horse's back, returns in my mind. I see my father crawling on all fours on the wooden floor of our apartment in Germany. His loud voice laughs with spontaneous hee hee hees, ho ho hos. Just as easily the room fills with silences. More waiting for my father's return from maneuvers, and then a Christmas tree suddenly lighting up the corner with delicious smells and our antique grandfather clock chiming its early morning time.

As an army-issued place, the rooms looked the same as all the other enlisted men's apartments. Only the color of the couches and the kitchen's smells differed. Identical radiators hissed from under identical marbled window sills near the bunk bed I shared with my sister. I sat on top and stared out the window, looking to see who was playing and hoping I might live in these same rooms forever.

My mother sat at the dining room table of that same apartment and talked with her friends while my ears attuned to her every word. "Little elephants have big ears," she said. I knew if I didn't disturb her, she'd let me listen longer as she and her army-dependent women friends shared their late afternoons with cigarettes and talk.

When I came home from school, I often found her dancing in our living room. Her stack of 45's fell song by song down the fat tube of their center, and shee bop, shee bop, rama dama ding dongs flew into the air. She and her friends twisted and shouted and let Elvis under their skin as they waited for their husbands to cross over from the world of soldiering into theirs.

On good days, a sudden rush came as the clock got nearer to five o'clock, and my mother would put together a dinner I can still quote: steak and then banana pudding layered with vanilla wafers on paydays; black-eyed peas with ham hocks as the month progressed.

I said we left those rooms in 1963, but did I tell you how it felt to leave my friend Yoko Whitiker behind? Yoko, with her tall

American soldier father and her petite Japanese mother, loved to rearrange my dresser top. Did I mention how much I loved to watch her take all the objects off, shake out the dresser scarf, and then arrange the pieces as if she was designing a still life? No matter how many times she did it, I felt lovely butterflies in my chest. The butterflies flew closer and closer to perfection with each new arrangement.

My parents' bedroom across the hall from mine had drawers built into the walls. My father's gun collection lay in between the clothes of those drawers. Maybe because we were a military family, you guessed that. But did you know the guns lay next to nylon stockings, perfumed sweaters, and girdles made even for thin bodies like my mother's?

A sewing machine sat along one of their bedroom walls. My mother used the machine to sew on my father's uniform stripes, which he lost and regained like days turning into nights. One day he would be promoted to what the army called an E7, and my mother would carefully sew on another stripe, making sure to place it just so on my father's sleeve. Soon afterward the army would take away a rank — down to E6 as a punishment for a drunken car accident. My mother would pick up the tiny stitches sewn around the stripe, pulling the threads out one by one with her tiny scissors. And so the process continued.

Years later in another room across the ocean, I tried to sew myself a dress on that same machine but ended up calling my mother's friend, Jeanne Harpole, to finish it. I remember the green-and-white gingham shift, but mostly I remember the room I sewed it in. It was in our first house actually — did I mention it was brand new? It even had a dishwasher and a sliding glass door out to an empty backyard. The green backyard covered the North Carolina pink clay I knew lay underneath. My father described so often the pink dogwoods and the white pines he planned to plant that I saw them growing in the yard before they existed. My imagination was like that. Actually the trees never came. It was either the wrong season for planting or my father's unit got shipped to war before he had time to turn his imagination into a forest.

Before he left for Vietnam — I don't remember which time because the years have melted together so it's difficult to tell where one tour of duty began and another ended. Before he left — I'll try again – he and I sat at the kitchen table and looked first at the dishwasher and then out to the empty yard. I remember no one else was home. Maybe this was the last time I sat alone with my father and had a conversation. Words passed over the oceans later. Sure. But this might have been our last conversation.

I remember thinking my father might cry. He looked at me as if waiting to see how I felt, which would tell him how to act. I sat and listened in my stoic manner. Even though I knew already about pulling the heart's edges together, I feared its contents might spill out onto the new wooden floor.

I would repeat what he said if I could remember his exact words. But I can't. It had something to do with my mother's drinking and my little brother found wandering near the highway. Was it Raeford Road which led to the base? It's not important. You don't need to know that. I can't even remember what school year it was. So what good is the map?

The darkness of that room is difficult to explain, so I leave it out. I save the sunlight that fell into shadows across the table. I leave out how the room became cold even as the North Carolina sun heated up the empty yard. I don't even know what it was that faded from my life at that moment. After all these years, it's still difficult to know.

I know only that I learned to stuff fragments deep into my gut. I learned to divide myself up into rooms like the wall of shelves between the dining room and living room of the only house we ever lived in. But all those details aren't part of the whens and wheres I've explained. My story gets burdened with the visual and the smells I pack into capsules of time and place. Yes, a new school. Yes, another town.

The rooms of perpetual dusk – that time not day or night when we anticipate only the day's end – return in my dreams. This time it is the four rooms of the alleyway apartment my mother rented when my father left again for Minh Thanh, or was it Long Thanh? They remain without the lights fully on. Surely we owned lamps and bulbs. But I'm afraid their brilliancy might have revealed what we all worked overtime not to see.

A curtain hung across the archway between my mother's bedroom and the room with a television. I say television, but I don't remember ever watching it. Not one comedy show. Not even a news show. I've made no mental synapses between the war news flashes and my life. I separated them out long ago, believing there was no war. No death. Only a room with a television and a couch draped with a thin, bumpy bedspread. The eerie light between day and night. None of it's on the map.

My mother's double bed sat surrounded by clutter on the other side of the curtain. Laundry baskets filled with clothes no one felt like ironing and cardboard boxes stuffed with things we never unpacked blocked the entrance. But maybe they weren't there at all. Maybe they were an illusion like the one I held then — that my father would return and we'd get on with life. Or the illusion about disappearing — that I could squeeze in and out of memory untouched by its caresses.

If I could only capture the room's smells you might better know the places that lie under the map. If I could make the smells come alive maybe you'd know why our conversation isn't important. Was there a cat food smell from all the strays my mother took in with her lonely heart? Or bowls of cold oatmeal still left on the table after school? And what does dust, heavy with dampness, smell like?

Or was it that the daily smells were so normal and that's why I can't recapture them? Is it only that I can't describe the smell of love fading like the light from outside? Or the smell of my mother's life tumbling into small crevices as she struggled each time to climb out.

The cry I bring out of those rooms can still be heard when my memories converge or it rains just so. When certain songs dance out of the radio and fall into my lap, I instantly recognize that era's rooms. I cry as though I'm still there staring out the window, waiting, rearranging my dresser top, hoping for the perfect layout.

To dwell there is to complain. I'm not complaining. I write to understand why hunger washes over me in the loneliness of dusk. I write to put the rooms to rights, as my grandmother would say. I don't want simple whens and wheres to answer questions that only stories begin to touch.

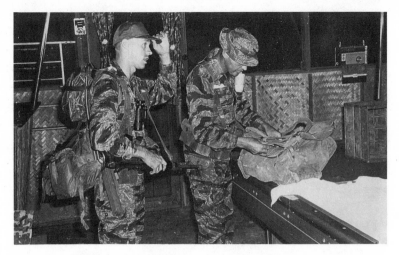

"Oct. 1965, Lt. Davis and myself prior to departing on operations."

Danger

My father wrote 0230 hours on the back of this Camp Minh Thanh photograph. I imagine the air was still then and that there was a quiet like the kind you hear when you get up in the middle of the night to prepare for a fishing trip. Only here, land mines and hidden enemies waited outside in the jungle. Bullets appeared from the dark, and bodies disappeared. Inside a hut of woven walls, my father (right) and Lieutenant Davis prepared to go out in the field near National Route 13. Certainty filled the air as they checked the details of their gear. I imagine the crickets outside talked under the bright quarter moon.

Harry McGloughlin once told me that my father was an absolutely fearless man. "There wasn't anything he wouldn't do or try, Gail. He wasn't afraid of physical danger itself."

Maybe this was my father's domain, his place of safety — within danger itself. It was the perilous uncertainty outside of danger, like family and home in times of peace, that was my father's Achilles' heel.

"Memorial Service for Sgt. Haywood, Camp Minh Thanh, Vietnam, November 1965."

A Form

To whom does this photograph belong? Should it be the possession of Sergeant Haywood, the man whose death is being memorialized here? Or how about the Protestant chaplain who conducts the service with his Bible in his hands? Or should it belong to my father, one of the somber, silent onlookers staring at the ground? I think of what Kafka once wrote: that we photograph things in order to drive them out of our minds. I wonder who the photographer was. Why did he take the time to photograph this moment? And why did it come finally to rest in my father's album?

After my father's death, my grandmother received a letter from a chaplain who had conducted my father's memorial service in Vietnam. He wrote that the Green Beret chapel was filled to overflowing that day with men who respected and loved my father. Years later I showed the letter to someone who casually said it was just a form letter. I burst into tears, quite by surprise. *No*, it wasn't a form letter, I wanted to yell. It was *my* father. *My* loss the chaplain addressed. There is no form to contain that.

December 1965, Hugh O'Brien, RVN

ven television's Wyatt Earp has come to the action of Vietnam — this theater of war — to entertain the troops for Christmas. It's difficult to tell the difference in this photograph between his toy gun and the real pistol hanging from my father's canvas belt. The edges of fact and fantasy blur together just as they did in the Westerns of my youth. Here my father stands, merging with the archetype of a soldier and looking as if he is standing outside time and place with this mythical cowboy.

Christmas of 1965 found my mother buying a plastic Christmas tree for the corner of our small apartment in Harrisburg. It was the first time we didn't have a real tree. Bulbs hung on it like strangers to the holiday. We decorated the fake, brittle tree with tinsel and tried hard to forget my father's absence. I saw my mother's eyes, and I swore I'd never marry a soldier.

That school year, my class chose me as a homecoming queen's attendant at my new high school. I sat on the back of someone's convertible, waving to the parade crowd. I danced in the queen's court to the Beatles' songs, "Help" and "Yesterday," and wore a prom dress for the first time. Long white gloves reached above my elbows. I smiled as one foot stepped into the real and the other into the unreal.

I have been dancing in and out of these two worlds ever since. Sometimes in the middle of shopping or sweeping the back porch I stop and superimpose a war scene in my mind on top of what we'd call normal everyday living. But war is not a common place, Robert Creeley wrote. And neither are the bombs I suddenly hear, the people running for cover, nor the nasty noises of death. Planes fly above me, soldiers march by, and I feel for a moment that I've been here before, that this is something deeply embedded in my life's history. This juxtaposition I carry in my mind is strange, eerie, and sometimes I'm not sure which part is real and which is illusory.

In another photograph I come across in my father's album I see John Wayne standing in a crowd of soldiers. He stands out with his height and the big smile that comes across his face, as if he is posing in a movie. He puts his hands on his hips while the other soldiers hold tight to their rifles. I know he isn't thinking of death here — not his own or theirs. He is only the symbol of the fighting man — the bigger-than-life soldier. I don't blame him for that, nor do I hold it against him that he will return home shortly when this visit is over. At least he is there trying to bring comfort and familiarity to these men so far from either. He wears a green beret, and I know that the real Special Forces soldiers did not do that while they were fighting. It would be a dead giveaway, a ticket to a target. In the middle of battle, they will not be able to walk away to "the world" the way John Wayne will.

Late-Night Photographs

own so few photographs of my mother. Those I do own are from my childhood with her on army bases: Fort Campbell, Kentucky; Fort Bragg, North Carolina; Flint Kaserne, Germany. The photographs capture our roles — me, her first child, her first daughter, and she, my young and fair mother only sixteen years older. It's like looking at a child playing with her doll.

It was my father who took these photographs. Long before I became aware of its flash and snap, he joined us together for poses. His frame went around our lives: these are my children, this is my wife. Looking back, I see his camera desperate to contain our lives, as if he feared he might lose them. His three little girls lined up, more often than not wearing identical dresses, with his young, beautiful wife standing behind them. She followed his camera willingly, as if she knew no other choice.

My mother was beautiful to photograph. A well-proportioned body. Flawless Irish skin that burned easily in the sun. Thick brown hair filled with curls. I want to say auburn hair or maybe chestnut brown hair, but the truth is that I am not sure. The black-and-white photographs of those years don't show it. By the time color photographs came around for the layman's use, she had dyed her hair black, so I don't know her true color.

People have told me that my mother was innocent. That she was a gentle soul who was in constant silent awe of the world. It's probably not easy for anyone who's heard some of my mother's later life history to imagine this raw innocence. But I know it was

"Gloria on Walken See, Bavaria."

there contained in her easy touch, her sometimes sad blue eyes. I knew early on that she would need protecting, and I didn't know how to do that.

My mother was different from any of my friends' mothers. First of all, she was younger. Younger than anyone's mother. I knew it. She knew it. It embarrassed me as a child. It seemed to me that an older mother might be more wise to the world, need less protection. While other mothers baked cookies – or so I fantasized – my mother danced to her stack of 45's and went to Elvis Presley movies. While other mothers made beds and cleaned their apartment, my mother went to have her ears pierced. While other mothers went to bed early so they could make a good breakfast for their family the next morning, my mother was sledding in the moonlight in our backyard.

Some of the photographs show her adolescent spunk, like the one of her and her sister, my Aunt Shirley, all dressed up and posing their best for the camera. Or the one of her and my father out-side the enlisted men's club on base: tight-fitting dress and high heels ready for dancing.

But in most of the photographs, I see a girl trying to do it right. Her three little girls, scrubbed and clean. Their blond hair combed. Their shoes buckled. The camera shows her with this re-sponsibility. Rarely apart from it.

Place, as well as people, are important in my father's pho-tographs. My mother in Naples, Italy. On Napoleon's highway near Sistéron, France. On the Riviera. A picnic at Tegernsee, Germany. A girl off the farm thrusts herself into the corners of a world com-pletely foreign to her.

Sometimes it's difficult to imagine my mother in all the pho-tographs' places: standing next to Juliet's tomb in Italy, on a gon-dola in Venice, or at an army ski resort in the German Alps. It's as if I am looking at someone else. She was a young person who, be-fore my father, never left home or poverty. Yet somehow she fits right in the photographs' edges. No one would blink twice to see her standing in places she never got to study in school. Shyly confident, if such a thing can seep through paper, revealing itself even after all these years.

I try to put together her face, the places, and what I know about her future, but it doesn't go together. She doesn't appear to be the woman who will die at age fifty-four, standing at a kitchen sink. Her apartment lacked what the woman in the photographs deserved. Not even a window over the kitchen sink. Not more than a box of belongings to call her own.

In the days of the photographs, my mother wore "Worth" per-fume from France. It sat in a little blue bottle on her dressing table next to her Chanel #5 and Joy perfume bottles. She wore silk stockings, lace slips, and Spanish high-heeled sandals. She loved dresses that hugged her thin body, red lipstick, and her aquamarine birthstone ring. Her short, soft fingers smelled of Nivea cream.

When I think of my mother, I think of her image in Europe be-fore my brother was born and life slipped downhill. I see her posed for my father's camera. Content and stable. It's difficult to call up other images, as if I'm afraid to witness the change. After all these years, I want to stop the camera before her world falls apart.

A photograph that was never taken remains in my head, its sharp edges coming together in the form of loss. Loss that no camera could capture. Twenty-nine years later, I awake, startled, in the middle of the night, my heart a mass of bloody pain that will not let me go. Lines verge, crossing each other in one large black point.

It is March 1963. My father's camera remains with him in Europe. I sit in my grandmother's American kitchen on a yellow vinyl dinette chair. The stove and refrigerator are but an arm's length away. A porcelain sink, low and large and flat at one end, reveals the kitchen's turn-of-the-century beginnings. Stairs lead down to the basement, where my grandfather's punching bag and old tools remain long after his death. A string hangs down from the round fluorescent bulb on the kitchen ceiling.

I became thirteen in that kitchen, but not before my parents separated and we left my father in Europe and entered the civilian world without him. I brought only my rock collection with me, hoping to save something of the earth that would not dissolve. My rocks held history, streaks of the earth's memory, and flecks of movement that once was.

In a few weeks' time, I lost a day-to-day relationship with my father, the protected environment of the fortress, and a European culture I had come to know better than that of the United States. I lost my childhood and then my mother's gentle presence when she left us to go live with her parents six states away. It seems my mother felt she needed to leave most of her responsibilities behind then. In Europe I had played with dolls, ridden my bicycle, and staged endless hours of Japanese dress-ups with my friend Roxann Castleberry. In my new American school, girls wore stockings and lipstick and went to Friday night social dances, a leap I struggled to make. It was a year to forget, only I can't. Its image stabs me in the middle of the night when there's no place to run, no defenses to hide behind.

The camera took few photographs of our life together after Europe. My father returned to the United States only to be sent to Vietnam. We took no vacations, no Sunday walks in the countryside, and life assumed a seriousness we hadn't had in Europe. War was no longer a practice maneuver but in fact a real thing where people like young Frank Badaloti died. The yelling and name calling between my parents flared up, and my father used his camera now for places he could never share with us. The time is a blur.

I am suddenly back in my grandmother's yellow kitchen with the string hanging down from the ceiling. It is March 1967. The kitchen fills with plates of food. People mingle and come in and out of the room. We are there for my father's funeral, a gun-saluted funeral. No one takes any photographs.

Now my mind snaps on the image of tall soldiers wearing their class A dress greens. A flag folded into a triangle passes from soldier to soldier until it arrives in my young brother's arms. Guns go off into the crisp spring air. Men salute. The heavy casket is lowered. Uncle Bob folds his head into his sobbing chest as if he just now realizes the final word. My mother stands silently, staring at the ground. Her lost pose becomes more familiar to me every day.

My mother's life had already changed before this parting. She stopped noticing her daughters' unbuckled shoes. She wasn't around to iron the identical dresses or to pose for photographs. She lost her way when the camera stopped clicking and found herself in a world of alcohol and "nerve pills." In a place with no paths out, as if they had disappeared off her map.

Years of such a life spiral down until she fell into an abyss and, for the life of her, could not get out. At fifty-four, she died at that kitchen sink. In a hot, lonely apartment without a phone. A box of belongings in the closet.

It wasn't what my father's photographs of her would have ever revealed. Maybe in that way, the photographs lied. They were in the end only what they were — frozen moments to observe. Moments that died the second the camera clicked. Moments labeled and then laid out between an album's covers.

In the late night hours, years and years away, I awake with a start to see a river, more ancient than memory, pouring down a mountainside, picking up melted snow. It flows over walked-on paths and cuts into the earth until new paths are made, bigger and deeper. The river opens its mouth, hungry for what it can't have, asking questions it will not answer. The answers push along over ancient stones, around bends I cannot see. As they echo, I run along, even as the river runs ahead. Porous words float along its surface, like photographs coming to life in a developing bath.

M. Sgt. Charles Ernest Hosking Jr.
Photographer: Bill Carlock, Carlock Studio, Ramsey, New Jersey.

Beating the Drum

Before my father left for his last tour of duty in Vietnam, my grandmother insisted he have a professional photograph taken. He wasn't interested but agreed just to please her. When he came to visit her before leaving again for Vietnam, he walked down to Bill Carlock's Photo Emporium on Main Street clothed in his full dress uniform. Tom Dater, a writer and an old school friend of my father, happened to be in the studio that day. He wrote a piece for the local newspaper after their meeting. In the "Beating the Drum" column he described what my father had been doing since he left Ramsey years before. He wrote of my father's matter-of-fact way of discussing weapons, jungle snakes and leeches, or Vietnam and that he did not speak of what he had personally accomplished. What struck Dater when he left to go back to the office was my father cautioning him to be careful, indicating the Main Street traffic. Both Carlock and Dater smiled over his concern, for here was a man who had fought in and was returning to a nasty, grubby war. Dater ended the piece by saying, "His name is Charlie Hosking and we have known each other since we were kids; he lived on New Street and I lived on Wyckoff Avenue. I wish him all sorts of luck."

Years later I got out my magnifying glass so I could scrutinize every insignia and patch that I thought I knew by heart. What brought me to tears were the words "De Oppresso Liber" written on his green beret. I knew the Latin words meant "free the oppressed," and I knew in that instant why I had been drawn like a magnet to the human rights organization, Amnesty International. I understood why I had written so many letters for prisoners of conscience, hosted garage sales, passed out leaflets for strangers I would never meet. In that moment of tears, I recognized that I had been trying to be the warrior my father had been. I was carrying on the mission. Finding the good war. Hoping to free the oppressed.

Echo Lake

In Hartwood, a place for hunting and fishing in the Catskill Mountains of New York state, rests Echo Lake, its tree stumps poking out of the calm, lily-padded surface. A few hundred-year-old boat houses come out of the forest and reach down to the water's edge. Their docks slant with age. Nearby, in an old stone house, *The Red Badge of Courage*, a book about the Civil War, was written by Stephen Crane around the turn of the century. Now beavers make their home on the shores, and when I am very still I can see a large bass or pickerel swim by. Not much has

"Fishing Echo Lake, summer 1966, Bob and Charles."

changed since a group of men bought this land over a hundred years ago before, they feared, it was lost to civilization.

In the summer of 1966 my father, on leave prior to his last trip to Vietnam, and Uncle Bob come here on a day trip to fish. Just the two of them drive up from New Jersey in my uncle's white Ford Falcon sedan and begin early in the morning to fish Echo Lake. They make their way around the edge in an old green rowboat and through the canal surrounded by tall grasses and turtles sunning on rocks. There are no fish to be had until they come around to the other side. It is here, my uncle tells me, that my father catches the fish he holds on a string so proudly in a photograph my uncle took of him. My father takes a picture of my uncle as well, and my grandmother frames them both inside one frame. For years I see it on her wall and believe it is one inseparable photograph. When she finally takes the frame off the wall to give to me, I am shocked as two pictures fall out. It is the metaphor for the final separation of brothers that brings me to tears.

Nothing about either the picture of my father or the picture of my uncle suggests my father is going off to war or that my uncle tries to talk him out of it. No tense good-bye feelings rise out of this photographic paper like they once did from a photograph my grandfather took of both his sons before my father left for the Second World War. In that one I see my father's clenched hand, my uncle's sad smile, and the forlorn stare peering out from their eyes. There is finality in that photographic image, parting in its voice.

I have no photographs of my father and me before he left for war that last time. And even if I did, I wonder if the photographic chemicals would have developed what I never let my heart feel. I was too busy pretending to the world that war was routine, life was forever, and fathers could never die. Would the lens of the camera have seen through that?

Many years later, while researching this book, I sat in the kitchen of Uncle Bob's log house on Echo Lake. At the antique table Aunt Val had refinished, I looked out through the many windows at the tall rhododendron bushes and noticed a lone row-boat in the distance. My uncle prepared salade niçoise with great consideration at the kitchen counter. His back was to me as I asked him about my father. I had questions about some of the photographs I had found. "Where was Camp Shelby, Uncle Bob? Where did my parents get married? And when was the last time you saw my father?"

One question led to another, as one story led us further into talk. My uncle never turned his back once as he told about the fight they had on my father's last visit home to New Jersey in 1966. They sat in my uncle's living room facing the fireplace, sharing conversation after dinner. My father said he was planning to return to Vietnam for the third time. At that point, my mild-mannered uncle began to list the things my father should consider before making such a decision: "Your wife is falling apart, your children need you, you have a home in North Carolina! Why do you need to go? You are just running away from things! And who will take care of your life here when you get your ass blown off?" By this time, my uncle was screaming at my father, who confidently and quietly answered him by saying, "You will, of course."

"Did you think my father wouldn't return, Uncle Bob?" I asked.

"His chances grew slimmer with each tour of duty. But I think your father was bound for self-destruction, Gail. If anyone was going to do it, it was your father."

He was right. Only a matter of months into 1967, my father's body returned to New Jersey in a black plastic body bag and was laid in a closed casket in the Van Emburgh Funeral Parlor in Ramsey just down the street from his childhood home. On the casket sat the eight-by-ten photograph my grandmother had insisted he have taken. It was now the month of March: my seventeenth birthday, my mother's birthday, my parents' eighteenth wedding anniversary, and spring.

At the graveside in Paramus, New Jersey, near the old Dutch Reformed church, where the bones of Revolutionary War soldiers still rested near its foundation, I recall Special Forces soldiers in full dress uniform standing in the background as they gave a gun salute. I remember the sound of their rifles being slapped by white gloved hands. I remember the stillness of the air. The American flag that draped the coffin was folded into a triangle and handed to my then-six-year-old brother. The family huddled with shoulders and heads hung low under a canopy. As Reverend Highberger spoke, I looked up to see my Uncle Bob rest his chin on his chest and burst suddenly into sobbing tears. I had never seen him cry before that. Nor have I since.

Just three months after my father's funeral, my sisters and brother and I went to live with my Aunt Val and Uncle Bob. My mother could no longer take care of us. I remember calling my uncle one night in the spring of 1967 from a neighbor's phone in the housing project where we lived. I was crying in despair, not knowing what to do. It must have been the next day when he flew into Evansville, Indiana, and drove to Harrisburg in a rented red car like a knight in shining armor.

In the few days he spent with us, he made plans to have us come live with him once the school year was over. He bought each of us some clothes from a store in the town square and then flew back to New Jersey with those plans. I remember taking a very deep breath as if someone had just saved my life.

Mrs. Coon, a social worker in town, assigned my three siblings and me to families to live with in the interim. "People will be good to you in a time of crisis," I remember her saying. "But they will help out for only so long." Sometimes even now I find myself measuring tolerance, observing limits, wondering when the moment of impatience is going to set in.

But then I think back to the time my father found refuge during the Second World War with a French family in the mountain village of La Bollene Vésubie. It's too small to be found on a map, but that doesn't mean it doesn't exist. I know because I went there once with my parents when I was five years old. It had been a decade since my father had seen them last, but memory and an unspoken thanksgiving for their care drew us back up the mountain to find their village. My mother and I waited in the hot car while he looked for this family. I remember seeing my father walking toward our car with a stranger's arm around his shoulder. They spoke French together and laughed like old friends. After much food and smiles, our families stood together under a balcony between two stucco apartments as if we were posing for a family portrait. The photograph remains in my father's album as a tribute to the kindness of others.

In June 1967, my sisters and brother and I arrived at the Newark Airport. Aunt Val and young cousins Debbi and Patti met us at the gate. Right away my aunt took us under her wing like a mother duck. On the way to our new home, she stopped at Sears and bought us each a bathing suit so we could go swimming that evening. She bought furniture at garage sales, borrowed beds, and spent the summer refinishing furniture in the garage. We folded laundry together in front of the television while we watched a soap opera called *Days of Our Lives*. My uncle left each morning for New York City and arrived home late each evening. All six children vied for his attention as he walked through the door.

I began my senior year that fall at Northern Highlands Regional High School, my twelfth school in twelve years. I looked like any girl next door. I lived with silence about the war both at home and at school. My aunt and uncle were practical people, and they put their energy into practical things. What size pots will feed a family of eight? How many eggs do we need for breakfast? Whose turn is it to do the dishes? Who took the garbage out last? Did you put your clothes away?

One morning as I stared into my closet trying to figure out what to wear to school, I felt a tremendous sigh of relief in the very core of my body. For the first time, I understood the stirrings of what it was to be a teenager, not an adult. Tears formed in my eyes that morning as I realized what a luxury it was to struggle

over clothes. At other times I would sit on my bed and cry for reasons I couldn't explain to my aunt or myself. She would try to talk
with me, but my silence would eventually drive her out of the
room. A rage would overcome me and I would want to scream,
but all I could do was ball up my fists and cry.

Mostly life went on as I imagined it did in any suburban civilian family. All eight of us passed food from right to left around the
table in the L-shaped kitchen. We looked out the latticed windows to see red roses my uncle had planted to climb on the rail
fence. We ate breakfasts of scrambled eggs, kippered herring, and
baked beans. Snowflake, the cat, bounced at our feet, and Sarga, a
Hungarian vizsla, played with a ball in the yard. After breakfast,
we piled into the car we called the BGC – the big green car – and
I drove my uncle to the train station. He got out, clicked his heels,
and announced, "Illegitimus noncarborondum," meaning, don't
let the bastards get you down, as he walked toward the train looking like all the other suited men with attaché cases heading for
New York. Then I dropped off each child one by one at their
schools. Their lives blurred by mine as I was finding my own way.

How one weaves together two separate families is complicated.
How cousins become sisters, how an aunt and uncle become parents even when we all know they aren't, is something of novels,
fictionlike. It comes when there are no other choices and when
the hearts of all open wide to include more than they had planned
for. Only years later, when I housed two teenagers of a college
friend, did I suddenly realize just how difficult it must have been
for my aunt and uncle. As I watched my two sons struggle with the
new shape our family had to take to include new people, I realized again how difficult it must have been for my cousins.

I had pulled up a chair at their table. I took up time with their
parents and watched their television. I never said please, I need
this because . . . I just came in and began sewing A-line dresses on
my aunt's, their mother's, sewing machine. They were young then,
and I was envious as I sat on their beds listening to their Monkees
records and admiring their dolls lined up against the wall. I never
thought of the changes they had to make in their lives. Not for a
second. I was circling within my own head, and my own loss was
all I could fathom.

Debbi, the oldest in her family, became the middle child when

I arrived on her doorstep that summer. Overnight, we all lined up, and she lost her place in line, moving back three spaces before anyone noticed. I remained first in line, the oldest of all six children, and I slept across the hall from Debbi while she moved into her sister's bedroom. We never spoke about the war, why we had come, or what life had been before. I was to learn decades later that silence did neither of us good.

When we were all grown, my sisters and cousins and I sat one late evening on the floor of my aunt and uncle's Hartwood home. Surrounded by antiques, woven Navajo-style pillows, and wainscoted walls, we sipped on fresh peach daiquiris and joked about our unique family life. Someone had put eyeglasses on the deer's head on the wall, and it made us all smile just to look at it. When the clock slipped by the midnight hour, a question came from across the darkened room: "What did you think, Debbi, when you suddenly got a new family back then?" The room grew very still.

"No one ever asked me that," she said.

It was precisely at that moment that I recognized for the first time her lonely, silent heart. I wanted to go back in time and ask her that question, to talk about the Vietnam War, my mother's drinking, and life in twelve schools. I wanted to thank her for providing the form I slipped into just as I was fading. But all any of us could do at that hour was to sit and stare and feel the heaviness of the air. Debbi looked down into her drink, quietly twirling the ice cubes around with her finger.

Again, years later at a Christmas gathering, another moment of recognition. My uncle showed me photographs of Debbi's paintings she had recently sent from Hong Kong, where she was living. I admired the pictures as I looked through the pile, and I commented on her being a good artist. One photograph near the end of the pile stopped me much the way that Hartwood midnight moment had. My father's Medal of Honor was painted in the middle with concentric circles superimposed over it like a firing target. Red paint dripped down like blood. Lines like bars were drawn over the medal. And finally, in the lower right-hand corner, she had painted shadows of young figures.

These days Debbi has moved to Paris, the site of peace negotiations for a war that changed both of our lives. Her belongings remain in the port of Hong Kong because of some bureaucratic detail. She reminds me of my father, who was more comfortable out of our country than in it. She devotes herself, like my father once did, to her work.

The family gathers at Hartwood for my grandmother's one hundredth birthday. The house is filled with the results of our growth — over twenty people now, counting husbands and children. We crowd into the kitchen and drink champagne Patti has bought, the appetizers I have brought, and the French cheese Debbi carried in her suitcase from Paris. We wait as we did years ago for my aunt to complete dinner. The only difference is that now my retired uncle helps prepare the gourmet meal for the crowd. He shoos us into another room so he can cook in peace. We go to the living room and sit around the stone fireplace as we make toasts to my grandmother and to the chefs. We speak about taking a trip to Vietnam together someday. Echo Lake sits outside the window. A lone rowboat with a single fisherman floats by in the distance.

Bien Hoa

Al Arellano told me about the time he arrived at Bien Hoa in Vietnam in 1966. "I got there and couldn't find a place to stay right away. Your dad saw me and told me to bring my gear into his room, which was located right off the bar. Lots of Special Forces guys had rooms there. He asked me to come and have a beer with him. We sat down at the bar and this monkey came up to us. He must have belonged to the bartender. The monkey hated your dad for some reason, and your dad hated that monkey. We got to laughing and drinking, and your dad got out his pistol and threatened to shoot the monkey. He never did shoot it."

In a photograph taken the year before Arellano arrived at Bien Hoa Air Base I see my father standing outdoors with a lift machine behind him. If nothing were written on the back of the photograph and if it hadn't been taken out of his album of Vietnam, I would think he was posing for a Hollywood movie set. I can imagine someone off to the side yelling "Move it over there. Everyone have their places? Ready? Roll!" And in walks my father, beret in hand, field uniform sleeves rolled up, dirty jungle boots, rifle in one arm, and mail in the other.

It's the mail from home juxtaposed with the weapon that best sums up my father. His was the life of both, trying somehow to maintain each as if that were a perfectly normal way to live. He has in his hands what he wanted most — his family and the army. What the photograph can't reveal is what writer Michael Herr calls the "survivor shuffle," which my father must do constantly in order to stay alive in both worlds. His alternating attention must have spun him around at times in some unnatural east-west interface. It was the world of *hoa binh*, Buddhist chimes ringing for peace, as bombs dropped all around him. It takes a strong mind to separate out the two worlds, drawing lines where one ends and the other begins. Or was it that after a while it all blended together for my father — one scene, one life?

In this photograph he looks insecure in the role he must play as if there aren't enough clues around to tell him how to act or what to say. No bullets or trip wires to look for, no incoming helicopters to direct. No adrenaline flows in this picture. Nothing evokes the feeling of walking on a ledge high above an abyss, nothing of life on a purely physical plane. It looks as though my father were dropped with his gun straight out of his isolated jungle camp right into the ease of civilization. Perhaps that is how my father saw home from his world of war.

Friends

As far back as I can remember I saw my father with friends. Their names spilled off the top of his tongue, filled our apartment with drink and laughter, and spread themselves out between the covers of his photo albums: names like Joe Dillon, Chucky, Elroy, Jack Worsfold, and George Pernak. As they pose for him the albums fill with more names of strangers I never met — Deacon in Cedar Creek and then in Philadelphia, Steve Halik and Teddy Hundeman in 1945 at the Colonial Inn, Fleming in Rome.

Some of the photos pinned down with red, white, and blue corners have faded as if they came out of our own Civil War. One that

Friends.

looks like tin is small and dark, and the layer of developed paper
has crinkled at its edges as if it's been in a fire. As it peels from its
black backing it looks as if I am seeing a spirit rising from the
photograph's strong bodies and leaving death in its wake. I can
barely recognize that it is my father. He and his friend Alonzo
Gappon stand somewhere in Montreal wearing Canadian army
uniforms with no insignias or markings to identify units. I wonder
as I look at this stranger if he has an album with a similar photograph, barely preserved and labeled, the details left for others,
like me, to comprehend.

As a child, I felt my father's friends took him away. I was jealous of them because it seemed he spent more time with them than me. Maybe it was this envy that caused me somewhere in my childhood not to trust men or made me feel that soldiers' lives were important in a way that could not include me. I grew to believe that only women would not leave me. It is ironic now that it is my father's friends who give me back my father. It is they who come forward in my time of need and give me stories to bring him back to life.

I can see now that my father loved this part of being a soldier: the camaraderie, continuous intimacy, and dependence unknown to the civilian world. In that way it isn't much different, I imagine, from the world of Catholic nuns or Buddhist monks. Here it is the world of men knowing men, counting on each other and sharing the mission of the surrogate parent — the military. This closeness with his fellow soldiers absorbed my father's life and made him feel at home in the strangest of lands. Friends gave him back the individuality the military robbed him of.

I see a soldier jump out of an airplane in a photograph taken somewhere over the skies of Fort Benning, Georgia. Then another soldier. And another. My father follows, and more come behind him, until the sky is filled with parachutes and men as if they are part of one big celebration, searching for a place to land. He, like the documenter he is, snaps a picture of each step along the way.

Years later, my father's Native American soldier friend, Elmo Clark, calls me and says that he "doesn't know what it was about Snake, but people just really liked him. He always had lots of friends." With that phone call I remember my father once telling me about the soldiers he loved and missed in Vietnam. Clearly he was at home among these men. They saved his life many times, he told me. War has a strange way of melting the barriers of race, class, age, and culture — all things that separate people in the civilian world. What remains are friends fighting for each other. It is this "boundless capacity for self-sacrifice," writes G. F. Nicolai in *The Biology of War*, "that is intoxicating about war."

Maybe it was this love my father felt for his friends that kept him from being suffocated by the power of the force of war, a force which can turn anyone subject to it into a thing. Back in 1940 Simone Weil asked, How does a soldier maintain his soul? How do you respect life in somebody else when you have to cas-

"12th December, 1966, Long Thanh."

trate yourself of all yearning for it? "It demands a truly heart
breaking exertion of the powers of generosity," she concluded.
Without it, the soldier becomes "a scourge of nature."

In *The Iliad* I read about warriors maintaining their souls in
war. Sometimes, like Hector before Troy, a man finds his soul as
he faces his fate "without the help of gods or men." And sometimes it is in a moment of love, like I think my father felt for
the comrades he saved with his death, "when a man discovers
his soul."

Future Past

W hat I notice about this Long Thanh photograph is
not my father preparing for a parachute jump with
some Nung soldiers but rather the date my father
wrote on the back. It lights up in an instant: the
date is three months before my father will be killed. I realize he
has no clue about that as he waits with the others. Maybe it's my
imagination, but I look at the three soldiers watching my father's
movements and I see one with his hand over his ears, one covering his eyes, and the other looking on with acceptance as if they

all already know what will be. Or maybe what I bring to this photograph is my own reluctance to see and hear what is coming. Maybe, like the third soldier, I observe the scene with helplessness because I am looking at both the future and the past at the same time.

In December 1966, I was interested in my boyfriend's football games and driving around town with my friend Dwana Kay. I memorized Latin vocabulary words, washed dishes in exchange for my lunch in the school cafeteria, and poured orange juice with the Girl Scouts at the Red Cross bloodmobile. I wrote fewer and fewer letters to my father. Our lives could have been on separate planets. I could not have begun to understand just what it was my father was doing so far away from me.

I look back and wonder what I thought would happen. Did I think the light would go on again the way it did after a sad movie? Or did I know by heart that tragedy was around the corner, so that choosing what color knee socks to wear seemed as important as anything else I could possibly think about? I don't remember speculating about my father's future. It might have killed whatever strength I had for the endless days of waiting.

Sometimes in the middle of a day now I stop and think that something dreadful might happen soon. I wonder what gestures, what signals around me might be clues to what will come next. I picture myself months ahead looking back, wishing I had paid attention, as if preparation is all that is needed to stave off the inevitable.

The Sacrament of Memory and Praise

n Saint Patrick's Day, 1967, four days before my father's death in Vietnam, his friend Mike "the Weasel" received an LP from his mother: the Clancy Brothers singing old Irish tunes. My father helped him search Bien Hoa for a record player, but when they couldn't find one on base, they went into town and found one at a Vietnamese bar. Picture it: the Clancy Brothers' music blaring while two sweaty guys in tiger stripes poured down beers and laughed until there were tears in their eyes. One was already in his forties, an old soldier for Vietnam. The other was much younger and would refer some-day to his friend as "the old man." The Vietnamese behind the bar stared at them. Maybe Mike talked about corned beef and cabbage and the Saint Patrick's Day parade in Boston. Maybe my father mentioned his English ancestors.

When Mike called me to remember my father's death day, twenty-nine years after the actual event, I mentioned that my father didn't have any Irish relatives. "Yeah, but he had a lot of rogue in him so he had to be an Irishman." Yeah, I said. You're probably right. Later, when we hung up, I remembered that the patron saint of my college was Saint Patrick and that I used to wear a green velvet skirt to the annual ball. Even the beer was green that night. We were all Irish for a while.

I spoke to no one about the war during college. I felt that what had happened to my father in a country I never saw wasn't some-thing to talk about. Instead I studied and danced, studied and danced, always with a feeling of living someone else's life. My bouncy pose through the campus masked all I buried: Saint Patrick at war, midnight, Special Forces, raw, absolute, painfully quiet, Vietnam, Vietnam, Vietnam.

Mike recently sent me a book about the Green Berets at war, a Mike Force patch with its black-and-white skull and crossbones, and a replica of the red, white, and blue scarf my father used to wear in the jungles. The one Mike sent me had been given to a veteran at Boston's 350th Anniversary Parade when the veterans were finally welcomed home.

He sent me as well a picture of him standing in a wooden bar-racks as he leans against an unmade bunk. The wooden slats be-hind him look primitive, like the kind my son sleeps next to at camp. Mike's got his tiger-stripe shirt opened to his waist, and his dog tags are showing. He looks like a skinny kid with rubber thongs on his way to the shower. On the back of the photograph he wrote: "with love and fondest memories of your father, the one and only Snake." It was taken in early 1967, right before the death neither of them knew was coming. He tells me each time he calls about the day he drove up to Bien Hoa after having been gone a few days. There was a sign above the entrance: Camp Charles Hosking (The Snake), and he knew in an instant that my father had been killed in his absence.

"You know what I'd like?" I said to Mike on the phone. "I'd like to go to Vietnam someday. I want to go with my sisters and check out the place. Maybe write about it." There was a pause on the phone as if he were filled with bittersweet memories. Then with a rise in his voice, he said that if he won the lottery he'd pay for all of us. I mean it, he said. I'll take you there where it happened.

Last Mission

"Your dad never went anywhere without his bodyguards. There must have been some special bond between them. Whenever your dad came in country, two or three of the Nung or Cambodian soldiers would find him and follow him everywhere. They carried machine guns. One bodyguard walked in front of him and the other behind him," said Jim Wild, a friend of my father and one-time neighbor in North Carolina.

"I always considered your dad a friend even though we didn't see a lot of each other. We weren't on the same team, but I saw him on jumps in the late 1950s in Germany, then at Fort Bragg, and of course in Nam. He could be talkative and unload whatever he was thinking, but otherwise he was a one-man guy — stayed to himself a lot.

"The last time I saw your dad was back in March of 1967. I just happened to be in the area and thought I'd come to the launch site where your dad's team was leaving for a mission. I just thought I'd come and say good-bye. Your dad came up to me, put his arm around me, and said, 'It's been nice knowing you, Bud.' It was out of character for your dad to do that. It was like he had a premonition. He smiled, and I remember his gold tooth catching the sun before he turned around and got on the helicopter. I never saw him again after that. I'll never forget him."

"Thach Sung, Tra Cu, March, 1967."

Tet Celebration

How and when exactly I came across this photograph of my father eating with chopsticks with sandbags and Vietnamese soldiers behind him, I don't remember. I found it when I was searching for something else to write about for a writing workshop. And then there it was staring at me, and I couldn't put it aside. Maybe it was the way it seemed my father's blank gaze saw through the camera and out beyond the noise and festivities that caught my attention. Maybe it was

Tet celebration.

the way it appeared as though he was looking at me with an ur-
gency, pleading with me to stop and look. I looked again that
night and wondered perhaps if he'd stopped spontaneously, with
his chopsticks somewhere between the plate and his mouth, and
realized as the camera clicked that part of him wasn't in Vietnam
at all, just as part of me was never fully where I was as long as he
was gone. Did he, for a few minutes, stare across the South China
Sea, out past the Philippines and Hawaiian Islands, and leap to
one of the many places I lived while waiting for his return? Did he
recall the egg salad sandwiches my grandmother made for my
lunch, or the macaroni and cheese my mother cooked for dinner
as he feasted at a Vietnamese celebration?

I went to his letters for details I once read but forgot. He wrote
about almost getting caught with a claymore mine near Cau Song
Be. How he had rushed his company at Tra Cu along the Oriental
River. "Got caught out in the middle of a rice paddy yesterday by
heavy machine gun fire," he writes. "This place is crisscrossed
with heavy marsh, rice paddies and cane fields — all dikes honey-
combed with fortification and mines. You stay wet. It is rough
moving. I was out swimming and paddling around in a sampan
with my Cambode bodyguard the other day."

It is only now, when I myself am a few years older than he was
when he died, that these details and photographs come to life for
me. Only now do I have the courage to really look. Now in my

middle-age years the whole scene wakes me up, and it's as if I am there, as if I can now know something about what he must have felt. It is strange, because I've never been a soldier, never carried a rifle, never depended on strangers for the safety of my life. Yet now I know about fear and duty and longing for the ones I really love. I know what masks he and I have worn in order to survive.

I go back to this photograph often now and wonder just what it was my father wanted to tell me, just what it was his eyes saw that mine never saw. Surely his stare had seen death before. But maybe, like the sandbags behind him, he built walls around his stare. Walls that kept him marching through savanna grass and bamboo thickets with land mines and viper snakes, crossing rivers full of leeches. Walls that kept him there and created a world so small it couldn't include me. Maybe the mask of those walls made it easier for him to go back, not once, but for two more times. Maybe it allowed him to take risks. Risks that finally brought him back in a black body bag.

Midnight Memorial Service

Last night at 12:45 exactly, I awoke and thought I heard my father's company commander, Capt. Jack Stewart, calling for help. He had just come to Vietnam as Captain Iacabelli's replacement and was now seven miles east of Bu Dop — that is to say, in the Third Corps of Vietnam. In the background of my dreamlike state, I saw only a dark jungle. "Help me," he called. "Help me." I couldn't reach him at 12:45 and not at 2:30 A.M. either. But still he called out with a sadness that has traveled over many years.

Three days before the Mike Force lost contact with him in Vietnam, he had witnessed my father's death and had come back to the base. He wrote me a letter then, dated March 23, 1967: "I haven't had the privilege of meeting you, your sisters or brother, but I did have the honor of having served with your father. I want you to know that we in the detachment truly respected and loved your father. I also want you to know that your father died so that two other men could live and has been recommended to be awarded the Medal of Honor. He was very proud of his children and you should be very proud of him. He loved you dearly and wanted only the best for you. Don't let him down. In all your future endeavors, strive to be the best as he did, and may God bless you for doing so." It was a typed, official-looking letter – the kind you barely read when you're seventeen and the kind at forty-five you're so thankful survived.

Last night I wanted to thank Captain Stewart for that letter, but I knew he wouldn't hear me. Only darkness surrounded his one-way voice in the early morning hours. "Help me." Not a firing weapon sound around, not a footstep, not even a bird watching in the trees above him.

I know from a list of missing Special Forces soldiers that his Mike Force Detachment A-302 company retreated from a battalion of armed North Vietnamese earlier that afternoon of March 24, 1967. Attempts were made to pick up Captain Stewart, but they were unsuccessful. The Mike Force eventually lost communications with him. The army calls it "missing in action," but no one knows for sure what happened to this man born March 30, 1941, in Washington, D.C.

"I'll tell them where you are," I wanted to yell out last night. "Just wait and they'll come to find you." But I don't know where seven miles east of Bu Dop is, and the Mike Force is gone now. There is no one to tell in the pain of predawn.

My imagination can only take me so far. I've not ever been a soldier or set foot in a jungle. I have no idea what real war is like. But logic remains: Capt. Jack Stewart would have found his way back to the Mike Force base if he could have walked. He would have devised a plan. I'm told that soldiers of the Mike Force were like that. Had he died on that spot in the jungle, his friends would have returned for his remains. But "missing in action" tells me nothing. Only that one more soldier is gone.

At 2:45 A.M., I hear his voice again, and I know something horrible has happened to Captain Stewart, something my mind won't imagine. I call to him: "I'm here. Hold on." But I know he won't ever hear me.

Capt. Jack Thomas Stewart's name is listed on the Vietnam Memorial Wall, panel 17E, line 40, thirty-five names after my father's. That's all I'll ever know for sure.

March 21

J ust writing that date out on paper has the power to bring up the past like an elevator rumbling up fast from the floors below without stopping. It's at once that exquisite relief of a winter passing and the hope that only spring can bring. It's memories of my mother's birthday and her dark curls and white, white skin. The way she blotted her lipstick on a piece of toilet paper. The way she let me play with the flesh on her arms as I sat in her lap. She was a toucher and always let us into her life that way. Like watching an older sister get dressed in her nylon stockings, hooking each one on her young thighs, I observed the feminine early on.

But coincidentally, March 21 is also my father's death day, now more than a quarter of a century ago. Still the calendar flips to this day, and something tightens inside me as if my muscles hope they can keep death away. As if in doing so, I can prevent some soldier I don't even know from knocking at my door and telling me what I know already. That same young soldier who found our apartment door back in March 1967 and stood there with the shiniest black boots, his regulation uniform, and his arms hanging down at his sides. His body image, never his face, has stayed with me all these years. So has that deep well of sadness I knew was in the air the minute I opened the door. It wasn't my own sadness I could feel that day but his, as if he had become in an instant the container for all I was incapable of feeling myself. I see him always like I'm flying above, watching what is now far away; and then suddenly I am there only inches from his tucked-in uniform pants, hearing the words he had driven from somewhere to tell us. In an instant he is gone, and I want to call him back to ask more questions, hoping he might be the one with answers.

I wonder only now about his ride into Harrisburg and his search for our housing project. Where he ate lunch and where he went when my mother wasn't home the first time he knocked. I wonder now about his ride back, what army base he returned to. What his thoughts were about us strangers. How he felt about the intimacy we shared for a few seconds: the announcement of death.

March 21, and I take a deep breath, letting it out slowly, hoping my muscles will relax as a Yahrzeit candle burns on the stove downstairs. The candle I've only in recent years begun burning. Not that it has anything to do with my father's Presbyterian / Buddhist life, but it's a marker for me, something to do on this date, something to remind my family that it still matters all these years later. That the man they never met really did live and then die on March 21.

The sun lights up the sky and peers through one of my bedroom windows, while a hazy gray fills the other. I wonder which way the day will go. This is March 21, always a blending of both. I hope I will not take to folding laundry, putting each piece in neat piles as if I were trying to neaten the stars.

Now, so many years down the road, there are questions that only in my middle-age years can I articulate. But the spring returns, and I know it's too late and that gone is gone.

CBS/Newsradio 88, May 23, 1969

"Wesley Hosking is eight years old; lives and goes to school in a comfortable New Jersey suburb. But today he is not going to school. He and his three older sisters and other members of his family are in Washington.

"Later this morning they will go to the White House where the President of the United States is scheduled to present to Wesley the nation's highest military award: the Congressional Medal of Honor. An only son, Wesley is accepting the medal on behalf of his father, Master Sergeant Charles Hosking, who in his act of bravery was killed two years ago on his third tour in Vietnam. Two years ago Wesley was six and they brought his father's body home and when they buried him, they went back to war.

"Sergeant Hosking has been a career soldier for twenty-five years. His medals included five Combat Stars, the Bronze Star, the Purple Heart, three Presidential Unit Citations. He had been a paratrooper and member of the Special Forces. In World War Two, he was one of thirty survivors of a unit which started out with fifteen hundred men.

Medal of Honor presentation by President Nixon, May 23, 1969.

"Two years ago, in a moment of bravery, he died. Today, the Medal of Honor. Posthumously. And what can we say to fathers who give their sons, or sons who give their fathers?"

Richard Reeves

May 1971, Hosking Field House Dedication

he army paid my way from college down to Fort Bragg, North Carolina, for the dedication of a new gymnasium named after my father. My siblings and my grandmother flew in as well. Once again, my mother was left off the guest list as if she never existed. It was an official sort of day with ribbons, speeches, and a large cake cut up and served to all the many guests. I posed near a painting of my father while cameras snapped the "official photograph." Little had my father known the day he went into Carlock's Photo Emporium to have his picture taken that it would one day be used for a painting of a mythical hero. Nor did he know that young soldiers who never knew him would one day play basketball and lift weights with this figure overseeing their actions.

The warm North Carolina day had a surrealistic quality to it, as though I was watching a movie about someone else's life. Being on an army base again was as familiar as an old friend and as awkward as a stranger. My feet were in two worlds now, the civilian and the military, and I hadn't yet learned to walk the bridge between the two. I went back to college and never said a word about this day.

Last spring, I returned to this gymnasium, bringing my husband and two sons. Neither of them had ever been to an army base before. Buildings had grown up around the gym, and it looked well used, as though it had been there forever. I was introduced as the daughter of the Snake to strangers who shook my hand. They showed me around like I was an old friend. The painting had, over the years, grown smaller as it hung in the entrance hall not too far from a sign that read "Weakness makes cowards of us all." I showed my family the plaque outside the building, pointed out the painting, and lingered, secretively thinking my father might walk through the door any minute.

Mētis

These are my secrets: I love people calling me "hon" even though it often brings me to tears and I don't know why. I dream that a white station wagon will finally drive me to safety. I rarely give up my vigilance, and I have no idea what it is I am waiting for.

Just the other night at a lecture by the Russian author Tatyana Tolstoya, I recognized this vigilant tension within me, as if only a part of me listened to her beautiful language glide over perfect word combinations. Another part of me tightened inside, wondering what was going on at home and who needed me — not that I don't have a right to listen to a lecture unencumbered from my responsibilities, or that anyone at home would be angry at me for leaving for a few hours. But still the vigilance remained.

Lately I am more aware of it than ever. Who knows why? But this I can say: I'm tired. I'm tired of feeling constantly in charge, of feeling like the world around me might collapse if I loosen my muscles. My body worries if I give in to the moment, as if I am anticipating tragedy and it is I alone who can forestall the future.

I found a photograph of my father my mother took thirty-four years ago in the backyard. In the picture, he sunbathed between two apartment buildings meant for U.S. army dependents stationed in Germany after the Second World War. I instantly recognized his plaid bathing suit, his gold watch, and his tattooed forearms. What surfaced slowly was what I had watched early on in childhood but only now can articulate.

In the photograph, my father still wore his shoes and watch as if he could never consider fully sunbathing. My father was on constant vigilance. This I know for sure now. It was his duty as a soldier and his only safety in war. Even on a summer's day away from an obvious war (only the more subtle cold war), he couldn't give up his vigilance. The camera captured what my body carries around to this day.

I feel like my father looks in that photograph — like I'm neither sunbathing completely nor am I at the guard post. I am caught somewhere between the two places, being tugged both ways at the same time. I have an eye toward life's pleasures while I am on guard and another eye toward the guard post when I'm enjoying myself. Like oscillating between two poles, I am ready like my father to go in any direction. It's an exhausting way to live, and I wonder sometimes if that's what really killed my father at age forty-two, not the grenade the army notice said. Whatever it was, his death was not from being caught off guard.

When my father went off to his final war, he left me with responsibilities I'm afraid I didn't fulfill. He asked me to take care of the family — to see that my mother wasn't lonely, that my sisters and brother flourished, and that my grandmother received letters from me. "Don't tell Grandma, but I have been on operation since January. We should be out by the Tet. The VC usually work out hard before the Tet."

In another letter he wrote: "Please help out your brother Wesley. I am sure you don't want him to be behind everybody in school." He spoke so naturally about sampans and MK rifles in the same letter. Then at a distance, he threw in "I love you" and "be a good girl."

I added up each request and carried them around on my teenage shoulders, afraid to put them down and confused about how to fulfill them. At fourteen, fifteen, sixteen, and seventeen, the years he was away, I lugged the responsibilities around even as I ran from them. What is left after all these years is the sensation of their weight, the fear of putting them down. I am caught with a watchfulness meant for war. I want to give up my vigilance, to quit being forever on alert.

All these years later, I am still trying to help out my brother, Wesley. Neither of us has much recollection of men lowering my father's coffin into the ground and handing a triangle-shaped American flag to my brother. Nor do we recall outwardly the years before that when I took care of my infant brother as if he were my own son. At thirty-four, he knows me only as his serious sister, the one who lends him, rent free, a room on her third floor.

"You're so serious," he remarked one evening recently as he did the dinner dishes, his back facing me. I was hurt at first, interpreting it as "lighten up." Then I grew angry and wanted to tell him I wouldn't be so serious if someone else would take over the family's vigilance. But all I could say in response was something about "I'm just thinking." I am, like the picture of my father sunbathing, still caught somewhere between feeling accountable and wishing I could get on with my own life. Mainly, I don't want to feel responsible anymore. Even so, out of habit, I look back over my shoulder, thinking I will make a difference. It's a habit embedded in my muscles.

When I was thirteen years old, my parents (after a six-month separation) drove up to my grandmother's house in a brand new white Ford Falcon station wagon. They picked us up and drove from New Jersey to our new home in North Carolina just outside the Fort Bragg base. I believed then that all was well again between my parents and that this new white car would drive us all to safety. Away from the cold war in Europe and the even more subtle wars within our family, I wanted to believe more than anything in the world that we could all let up our vigilance.

But it didn't work that way. Just as we settled into our very first house, talk of the Vietnam War filtered through our roof. As I rode my bicycle up and down Strathmore Avenue and discovered the Beatles, my father trained in secret for his next military mission. I thought when he announced to the family that he was going to Vietnam that I should never have given up my alertness —

that perhaps somehow I could have forestalled the inevitable had I only been on guard.

In the end, neither my father's vigilance nor mine saved his life. The ancient Greeks knew what I have suspected all along: that my father's act to save his fellow soldiers, the laying of his own body over a live grenade, was not impulsive. His momentary decision carried with it the full weight of his acquired experience. This informed prudence, or *mētis*, as the ancient Greeks referred to it, had become such a natural part of my father's warrior mind that he had committed his vigilance to the level of mere routine.

Maybe the ancient Greeks were right in believing that the man of *mētis* could look beyond the present and foresee a wide slice of the future. But what future my father saw in that moment of decision I will never know.

Sometimes it hangs over me — that one small moment of decision — and I wonder if the present is the future my father foresaw. Of what value are the words *mētis*, regret, and vigilance? I know, though, without a doubt, if only for a moment, that my vigilance will not save anyone. Nor will a white station wagon drive me to safety.

The Return

In the months before my forty-second birthday — the age my father was when he died — I felt a sudden pull toward Europe, in particular Bad Tölz, Germany, where my memories of my father were the strongest. The U.S. military had closed down Flint Kaserne just that past fall due to budget cuts, and I feared this place where we were once stationed would be written off the map.

I flew to Germany alone, with my notebook in hand, curiosity and memory in tow. My German woman friend, Gundi, whom I had known since my college days during the Experiment in International Living, met me at the airport and was my driver into the past. What irony, I thought, that a German, whose people had fought my father in the war and who had killed Jews, the ethnic ancestors of my Jewish husband, was now to be my partner for the next ten days in this search for my father. What I found as we pulled up in front of my one-time government-issued apartment was everything as it appears in this photograph of 1955. The apartment buildings were narrower and taller than I remembered, but they still stood in even rows going up the hill toward the American Army Dependents School as they had since they were built in the early 1950s. Except now the buildings were empty, since the Americans had left and the German government had not decided what to do with them. An eerie hush fell with the Bavarian spring snowfall.

When I got out of the car and saw a faded C-2, the number of our apartment in building 106, written on the parking space next to me, I remembered my father in that exact place bent over washing our blue Opel station wagon on Sunday mornings long ago. The sounds of my roller-skating past him came back, as did my memories of my sisters playing hopscotch or jacks on the sidewalk. I saw a long line of children waiting for their turn to use my red Hula-Hoop. Their eager laughs replayed as if it were yesterday, when I had begged my mother to drive the hour to the Munich Post Exchange for the Hula-Hoop I felt I couldn't live without. Now I ached for the revival of my family's life here in this small spot far from the shores of the United States. I searched the sky for a sign that I had really spent much of my childhood in this place. It was all here, I thought, long before I ever thought of marrying, having children, or writing about this life.

Our living room window was empty of curtains now, and I remembered as a child looking out from the other side to see which children were playing outside. Memories of King of the Mountain on the snow pile at the end of the parking lot came back as if the children had never left. I walked around to the back of the building and climbed up on the basement entrance's railings to peer into what was once our kitchen. Cupboard doors were opened as if waiting for my mother to return with groceries from the commissary. Family life, with my brother's high chair in the corner and ivy hanging from wrapped hangers my mother had made and then hung on the wall, reappeared in the empty silence of the room.

The quiet was so noticeable, it echoed off the cement fence that ran along the main road off to my left and behind what I had called "The Forest" as a child. Clearly it never was a true forest except in a child's imagination. I picked up a stick covered with lichen and a smooth stone and stuck them into my purse, hoping they would forever spark my memory of making forts and playing house under a canopy of tall, skinny trees.

What brought me to tears was seeing how narrow, almost nonexistent, the path down the incline alongside the buildings was now. "The black path," a childhood term known by all the children stationed at Flint Kaserne, the black graveled path my father walked every evening from his world of the army into our world of dependents' housing, had all but vanished. Time had worn it away. The path's disappearance reminded me, like only the solid, factual things of our lives can, that my father was indeed gone. I stood there catching snowflakes on my brown leather jacket. Tears streamed down my face as I wondered about memory and its ability to hold what goes away. I questioned what could happen when my own memory of this place faded. Would it float out into the universe, settling someplace I could never reach? Would it disappear into the pile of forgotten moments that history becomes? Would it become only and forever this story and nothing more? The ache was so deep I thought I'd never move from this spot again.

As I looked up again at the gray sky, I realized I had come to meet my father on this exact path, somewhere between his world and mine. It was here, in this land that belonged to neither of us, that we both had learned about fathers and daughters. I had returned to find that again after so many years away. I wanted to know what we do now that the path is gone. How do we create a new one? Where will my pen take me?

When I went inside stairwell C, more sounds and sights returned. I realized they had been close to my memory's surface all along, waiting to spill over. The flight of stone stairs led up eventually to the fourth-floor playroom, where I used to roller skate on rainy afternoons, driving Mrs. Lovell, who lived below, crazy. It was the same large room where I took ballet lessons from Frau Lilo von Solomon. I remembered how I begged my father for those ballet classes and how few enlisted men's daughters were there. It was unusual for my father to spend money like that on something he would have called frivolous, but he agreed anyway. Now, walking up the flight of stairs all these years later, I was thankful.

Along the way I saw the two apartment doors on each floor, the shiny green railing I used to slide down backward, and the button on the first floor which when pushed kept the lights on just long enough to climb the stairs. I wished that someone would answer if I knocked, and I could ask where I might find school friends, Arlene Jackson or Roxann Castleberry. But no one was there, every sound and every person gone.

I went back outside and stood in silence, not wanting to get back in the car, because I knew I might never have the chance to return again. Even if I could come back, this place might not be here, or else it would be filled with the immigrants who pour into Germany now that the cold war, a war my father fought long and hard, was over. I stood on the concrete stoop outside our stairwell where my sisters and I once played on hot summer days or that we used as base for our evening hide-and-go-seek games. I pictured my father cooking C rations out here as he once did, John Roy told me, on a portable stove used for maneuvers and not more than eight inches long. He was in full view of the neighbors, and that embarrassed my mother, who was angry at him and refused to cook his dinner that night. Roy told me that the guys would tease my father about this and laugh whenever there was a drinking occasion or Special Forces stories filled a room.

Gundi and I drove then over to the base that had been home to my father's Tenth Special Forces Group. We crossed the cobblestone street and drove through the arched entrance into the fortress that had belonged to Hitler's elite during the Second World War. I remembered having to reveal my dog tags before I was allowed to enter. Immediately I saw the square inside the fortress where soldiers once marched in time near the endless rows of windows looking out from soldiers' classrooms and barracks. It was a tiny world of America inside guarded gates. To see it again after so many years away was to experience the hunger of all that had been buried rushing at me with a speed I never imagined. I was disoriented for a few minutes, left floating between the world of yesterday and the world of today. I was numb. I wanted to touch everything, wanted to cry. But for a while, all I could do was walk around in a daze, lost in the desert of time.

I had to see everything inside the fortress and, like my father, take a picture of every place: the chapel, the officers' housing, the snack bar, the empty mess hall, the corridor between the post office and the newsstand where I used to run past off-duty soldiers, the paintings on the outside library walls, the wrought-iron gates to the commissary. I took a picture of the movie theater and then sat down where I had every weekend of my youth here. Memories of cartoons, westerns, and Sunday school group gatherings went on around me as I sat in the dark silence on a red upholstery seat. Nostalgia, I recognize, is seductive, and as I sat there wondering how time moves, how we get from one place to another, I felt a sentimental yearning, a childhood ache to return forever to this fortress. The desire to capture, a kind of owning of what once was, came over me. I wanted to swallow everything around me, as if in doing so I could have my father back. But only memory can do that. Only the unexplained mysteries of the mind can hold what goes away, not the objects or places of our past.

Gundi and I walked then to the motor pool where I posed near the Benzene sign in the exact spot my father had done back in 1955 wearing his Second World War 509 patch on his jacket. Trying hard to translate this all into German for Gundi, or into any words for that matter, became impossible as my tongue went to German then English and then back again, and finally I stood there looking up at the gray sky and my tongue went silent. I couldn't hold back the emotion any longer, and Gundi knew that. There we were, two women from totally different backgrounds, hugging each other and crying as the snow fell around us. We were what Hitler could never have imagined together: German and Jew, German and American — both of us daughters, both of us embracing.

We drove then out the arched entrance and up the hill where the last apartment building stood next to the Bad Tölz American Elementary School. This is the playground where I once got hit by a swing in third grade, I told Gundi. And here are the windows looking out at the airfield where planes took off and landed the whole school day and Mrs. Moffat had to stop her spelling assignment when all the army brats looked out. Here's where Miss Baker, the principal, had her office, and here are the flagstones I stood on as a safety monitor or when I waited to get into the gymnasium door. Nothing but the silence had changed. Even the dirt under the swings was ground in as if whole groups of laughing children had just walked over it.

We drove back down to building 106, and I got out for one last look. I wanted to stand there for as much time as it would take to memorize every blade of grass peering out through the snow or to see my father walking toward me on the black path. I was glad Gundi stayed in the car, because I wanted to be alone. I wanted to inhale the air like memory, hoping to possess this world again. At the same time, I wanted to step through the thin, delicate illusion that life never changes and find the woman I am on the other side. Gundi's patient waiting touched me. I took more pictures — the texture of the stucco, the side of building 106 where I had once posed for my father's camera with my brand new bicycle, the faded C-2 on our parking space. Sergeant Harpole's apartment was across the way. Sergeant Higgenbotham's was in stairwell A. A final photograph of the black path before the grass that surrounded it completely grew over it.

Finally I got back in the car after having taken more photographs than I had planned on taking. As Gundi and I drove away, I looked back over my shoulder for one more glance and tried to breath through the pain of leaving again. It was quiet inside the car for the longest time as she drove over familiar narrow German roads and I stared out the window next to me.

Sons and Daughters

his man I've never met — this Mike from Massachusetts who knew my father — calls me now and then. Sometimes I think I hear a drink in his voice. A lonely clash of cubes comes across the wire, and his smile, so big I can see it hundreds of miles away, is there as he speaks about "Old Snake."

"Your father was a character," he begins each time in his heavy Boston accent. "Jesus, what a soldier." Then he laughs a kind of private laugh, like he's back "in country" decades ago.

He told me about one of their times together in Vietnam after a "bucket party," where soldiers share a bucket of bourbon till their fallen comrade's memory blurs. The last one left standing puts the others to bed. This time my father asked Mike to join him afterward but never said where they were going. They drove a jeep into the night to the officers' club where the leaders of their dead friends and failed ambush were partying. "Wait here," my father said. He slid off the sweaty seat and ran into the building, only to return in a few seconds. "Let's get the hell out of here fast," he said to Mike, who drove away before anyone would know about the tear gas grenade my father had thrown into the officers' midst. "Bastards," my father said. "Bastards."

Last year Mike left a message on my tape machine the day before Memorial Day. I knew why he was calling. It was that time of year again when we remember those we swore never to forget from war. He wished me well, said he was thinking of me, and then mentioned the words "Memorial Day." My grandmother still calls it "Decoration Day," the day we decorate our war veterans. Mike called me to find his soldier friend, my father, again. I smiled as I heard his voice replayed on the machine. Then I took in a deep breath of memory and their friendship and the god-awful pain of missing people we once knew.

Father's Day follows Memorial Day, and I think of the Sons and Daughters who meet on Father's Day in Washington, D.C. "In touch" is their motto, their creed. They search for connecting memories – to find someone else who owns a folded triangle-shaped flag that once lay on their father's casket. They look, finally, after all these years, to hold the hand of someone else who knows.

After two invitations, I've not gone yet. Maybe I'll never go. I say it's the expense, the time, or the thinking I know all there is to know already about war. Sometimes I think it's not wanting to see all those people, the sheer number of attuned hearts all in one room. I fear it will remind me that my life, like my father's, is just a number. Just another grown child in a hotel convention room. Just another body returned in a bag, known only by its tag.

Sometimes I think I want to hold on to the memory of war. I want to keep it in one place so it won't happen again in my lifetime. I don't want my father's memory to scatter like the lives of all those Sons and Daughters after the weekend convention is over.

War is complicated, I would yell out to the Sons and Daughters if I did go to the Father's Day event. It's full of poetry, and life, and deep friendships, and horrors we can't name. It's full of death that still cuts across our view.

I would go wanting, like my grandmother, to decorate the fathers of the Sons and Daughters. At the same time, I would want to yell into their graves: WHY? Why did you leave us? What was it about duty and the dance of war that pulled you away on a rope stretched taut between here and Tay Ninh Province? What was it that's bigger than all of us which led you running toward the South China Sea?

Some Memorial Days I wonder, if I could have cried out my tears loud enough the year my father left for Vietnam, would he have heard my pleas? I wonder if he could tell me about a rage that still erupts now and then when I least expect it and clenches in my teeth and in my fists. Where does this feeling of wanting to kill come from? My body tightens like an AK-47 rifle before it shoots, and I want to explode like the grenade that finally killed him. It's as if I am like my father, continually mobilized for battle. Like soldiers driven to a berserk stage, I want to lash out at someone, I just want to kill. After my screams wind down and I'm resting the way I would after a long night's reconnaissance, my eyes close and the years get buried again.

I sent Mike a picture of me all dressed up in my best with a flowered maroon hat perched on my head. He pulled the picture out at the bar where he was sitting, he told me later, and showed it to everyone. "Looks just like the old man. Just like the Snake." He sent me some slides of him in Vietnam leaning up against the back of a soldier, his AK-47 on the ground next to him. Later, a package arrived with his beloved Mike Force neck scarf inside. He wanted me to have it.

On the opening night of a photo/essay exhibit about my father that I put together at city hall, a wreath of pine branches with a center candle arrived at the gallery. A red ribbon was wrapped around the whole thing with the words "In Memory of the Snake." It was signed "Mike, the Weasel. If you see a tall, uniformed soldier in the crowd, you'll know it's me." I half expected to turn around and see him walking in, half feared he really would, and the sight would surely bring me to tears. But he never did show up. His call the next day explained to me that "he just couldn't bring himself to come, but maybe someday." I understood the power behind his proposed gesture and at the same time I suddenly understood why it was I couldn't get to the Sons and Daughters convention.

"Oh, but your dad was a character. Jesus, what a soldier," he continues.

Conversation with a Blind Stranger Who Shines Light on the Forgotten

t is a strange thing to be speaking on the phone, sometimes for hours at a time, to someone you never met but who knows about part of your life. One soldier would call me with a memory and leave me with the telephone number of another soldier. I took footsteps across the country into places called Spring Lake, North Carolina; Remington, Virginia; Apple Valley, Minnesota; and Agspera, California. How could any of us have known that talk with the daughter of a fallen comrade or the fellow warriors of a father would be a reunion with the past of both of our lives, both mine and the stranger at the other end? Some of them were shy and had difficulty wading through what had happened "so long ago," and others spoke with confidence as they recalled stories as if they had happened yesterday. All of them were full of the courage it takes to remember the past or to call Snake's daughter. I took notes, fearing the soldiers' courage would fade and I would never hear from them again. What none of them could ever know, even when I wrote to say so, was just how essential their stories were to my writing and to the increasingly close contact I felt with my father. Each story was in its own way the act of meeting, each one a shining light on that which was once dark.

Buck Kindoll of Corbin, Kentucky — a name passed on to me by Jim Donahue, and a man now blind from diabetes — remembers discussing the Snake in a small room at Bien Hoa which was divided for privacy with a piece of board down the middle. He began with the time soon after my father had been killed:

Someone was saying that your father shouldn't be recommended for the Medal of Honor, that he would never get it and it was a futile gesture to recommend him. They argued that he had been in so much trouble over the years, had not played by the rules, so it just wouldn't happen. The guys carried on with the dispute for a while.

Major Skyles was sitting at a small desk in the corner of the room throughout this back-and-forth conversation. He was quietly filling out reports and went unnoticed by the rest of us until he suddenly jumped up on top of the desk and started reading those guys the riot act!

The major screamed at the other soldiers and said that one thing about your father had nothing to do with the other. "The man pulled off something that merits this award! And by God, he deserves it!" Then just as suddenly as he jumped on the desk, he jumped off and sat back down again to continue writing the reports.

Those guys were shocked and ended up saying that maybe your dad should be recommended for the medal.

No one hated Snake, but some wouldn't have done it his way. He was rigid about his high standards and, to tell you the truth, there was envy from others that he could do it — that he pulled off what he did in spite of his getting in trouble. The man could take weapons apart with a blindfold on and then put them back together again. He knew weapons like no one else — could write a weapons lesson plan from memory. He could be dead drunk one night and then awake with an automatic alertness as if there wasn't a drop of alcohol in his body. I saw him do it many times. You have to think about what he did in spite of his drinking. That's how you have to look at it. Your father took his soldiering seriously. And there's not a soldier alive who knew him who would deny that.

You have to understand, there was a tremendous intensity in your father's work. In Germany during the cold war in the fifties, the Special Forces did six weeks of Alpine ski training in the winter and six weeks of mountain climbing in the summer. During the fall maneuvers we spent a month going underground in the fields of Germany. We hid out and blended into the society — couldn't visit the compound [home] for that entire month. The Soviets had their weapons pointed at us at all times, and we knew it. We parachuted into places where we had no idea what to expect, and we often left in the middle of the night for missions. You didn't know from one day to the next where your life was going. Constant interruptions in your family life. You'd work all day and then get a call at midnight to leave. And the double pressure was that you couldn't talk about it. You can imagine it was a unique close community.

But everyone has their breaking point. The drinking was a planned break where you could let down. Your dad would get happy and wild when he drank. And maybe even a little more stubborn. I remember once at the NCO Club one Saturday afternoon when the MPs thought your dad had too much to drink and wanted to take him home. He went with them, but walked into the front door of his apartment and then out the back door and back to the club. He had lots of car wrecks too as I recall. Reckless. Lots of us were like that. The army wouldn't put up with it today.

Once your dad was in Garmisch, Germany, at the Olympic ski jump watching skiers go down. He was a good skier, you know. But he got to talking to a bunch of us guys and said he could go down that jump. In fact, it would be so easy, he had said, that he could go down in a box. And he did later that day. All he did was break his arm. What a character!

The tension didn't let up in Vietnam either. When the regular soldiers came in for the night in Vietnam, the Mike Force went out. Your dad was in charge of large groups of Chinese Nungs and Cambodes and he had them well trained, the best I'd seen. I remember once seeing him at one of the camps and he had the Nungs lay out their clothes so he could see what was going into their packs for an upcoming operation. He was counting their socks! That's how methodical he was. I remember asking him if he thought he would make contact. "What do you think we're doing all this work for, if we're not going to make contact?" he said.

Those Cambodes and Nungs loved your father. Whenever he came in country a few of them would find your father and follow him everywhere. His trademark in Vietnam was these soldiers with machine guns following him around — some in back and some in front of him. He'd even take them to the bars in Saigon and they'd wait outside for his protection. He took care of them too. It was a mutual thing. We had some Cambodes and Nungs who had retired and were thought to be disabled, but when they heard the Snake was back, they came out of retirement. They said if the Snake was back, they were back.

You see, your dad was one of a kind. He was disciplined beyond belief, but he could be equally as reckless. He had real respect for other nationalities. Very few ever reach the standard Snake did. You say you're surprised he wasn't killed sooner, but to tell you the truth, we were surprised he was killed at all!

You can't fully grasp it unless you've been there. What we went through, how we lived — it's difficult to explain. Civilians will never know. When you're trained like your father was, you feel a sense of self-worth when you're in combat that you don't feel in the peace-time army. There's a sense of importance that you can make a difference. And men like your dad were creative men — they didn't use a format to do things the way others had done before them. Each incident was different and demanded a unique way to look at it. The answers came from looking at things based on time and circumstances. Your regular army just wasn't equipped to handle that.

In the regular army you wouldn't see many retired soldiers calling each other by their first names either like they do in the Special Forces. The leadership techniques were different for us. Everyone carried their own load. Lieutenants would listen to captains who would listen to sergeants. The officers knew that the enlisted men were the technicians and that without them they couldn't operate. You were valued for what you could do for the team, not what your rank was. And you had guys knowing all the trades in the Special Forces. They'd read the basic manuals over and over again until they really knew their stuff.

People drawn to the Special Forces want to know everything that's going on around them. They want to know the exposure factor and all the information before they go out on a mission. But in spite of that, they still go. They have respect for others doing their job — know they can count on you to back them up.

But eventually you get to the point if you stay in combat too long you hang your head over the cliff for that sensation of extreme tension. You get to the point where you need it to be happy. It's never an easy transition back. Special Forces got emotionally involved in the country too. When you've got guys speaking the language of the country and you're working with the people directly, you start to feel protective of the place. And then when you go home, you feel like you're being left out if you're not back in country. You feel if any of your buddies are still there you need to be there to protect them. So you return again and again, like your dad did.

I still get calls from Vietnamese people who left Vietnam. And the Special Forces support the Montagnards — the Yards, as we call them — in this country. As soon as they come they look us up. You've got second-generation Montagnards now still looking to the Special Forces for help. There were lasting relationships created in Vietnam. The gap between their fore-fathers and here is unbelievable. You can't imagine!

The Vietnam War should have been a civil war, the way it really was in the beginning. We had no business intervening there. We should have just supported them. The politicians in Washington failed to see this, and in the end we did the fighting and the South Vietnamese became the bystanders. I went because I was a professional soldier and that's what you do then, but our country had no business there.

Now I'm blind from diabetes and waiting on a kidney. I've had my disappointments in life. Got to use that same Special Forces creativity to deal with it now.

Your dad was a good man. He worked hard and he played hard. He was the Snake!

A Bridge

My neighbor who collects images of bridges asks me for a picture of a bridge from my father's photographs. First I tell him that there are no bridge pictures. I could swear that since I've looked so many times. I still observe the photographs with a magnifying glass, which gives me the enlarging gaze of a child and brings a lump to my throat that's so big I think I will never swallow again.

Each time through the albums I find something I didn't notice before — like a jungle photograph with a punji pit pointed out by my father's pen, a photograph with a Song Be sign in the back-ground, or one with two unknown soldiers smiling for my father's camera. I suddenly remember him mentioning the Song Be River in one of his letters — the letters I read quickly, and then, in my self-absorbed world of adolescence, would run off to a school dance with friends. I wish now I had saved those letters.

This time through the albums I find two photographs of bridges shown off in the background. They both look as if an artist drew them in at the last moment to add interest and per-spective to an obscure landscape. I think at first that the pictures might not be photographically clear enough for my photographer neighbor and that I don't have the negatives. But I give one to him anyway, half fearful that to give any of the collection away is to lose something bigger than a small photograph of a bridge I will never see and probably doesn't exist anymore.

Another part of me longs to show everyone these pictures. I want to point out every detail about this man I catch myself writ-ing about as "Daddy." At the age of forty-five now that rings odd. It reminds me how we never got beyond my childhood together. He was killed before we made the leap into "Dad." I want to put life's noises back into the silent photographs. I want to say that these bridges meant something to my father's camera. I want everyone to know that he died near the Song Be River saving the lives of other soldiers. Maybe it was near a bridge. One that no longer crosses a river.

Untitled

find images I can't bear to leave out: my mother holding her third new baby next to my father's shiny 1953 Mercury outside Fort Bragg, a dark cloud of coal dust hanging above our Smoke Bomb Hill apartment, some young soldier on furnace detail shoveling coal into our bin, me and my mother posing out-side Juliet's tomb in Verona. I see my father stretching out his legs onto one of our rare non-government issue furniture pieces, a red Turkish ottoman. He looks mesmerized as he reads one of his blue basic army manuals. They are the same manuals Laudacina finds him reading in a hospital bed when he comes to visit him in

Saigon. In another photograph, I am sitting equally as still and absorbed while I read my book. The light from the window falls across the words.

I return to my father's albums, hoping to memorize each detail the way my father memorized those army manuals. I am deathly afraid I will lose him again if I don't. I grasp for more scraps of information, more illuminating stories, or another image I've missed. I look to construct an ending without that familiar feeling of loss.

At a certain point, my father's albums stop containing us. Instead, I see him at such places as faraway Wake Island. The flowers behind him sway in the tropical breezes near the coral inlets. He squints into the sun, and I imagine the Pacific Ocean roaring behind him. My father's face is the same whether the camera captures him here or in Germany, Alaska, or Vietnam. He wears the same fatigues, black boots, and chevron stripes. Wherever he goes, he hands his camera to another soldier and asks him to take his picture to send home to us. Be sure to get the big rocks in as well, my father says.

I notice he collects other unpredictable images in his albums: a Moslem mosque, a view of To Do Street's fountain, a Vietnamese funeral at Loc Ninh, the Tackikawa Air Terminal, and a woman and her child on a bicycle near the American consulate in Saigon. He captures street advertising, Vietnamese friends, and a lone sampan on the Saigon River. As if to confirm the nonaccidental nature of my father's years of collecting pieces of his life for us, his albums have more pages of him. In one such picture, I see him in a market strolling by women dressed in black pajama-style pants and cone-shaped straw hats. They don't appear to be paying attention to this blond stranger dressed in American civilian clothes. They are busy selling baskets of fruit, bolts of fabric, and pots and pans and don't notice this Special Forces soldier on leave from his isolated camp. They don't ask him where he left his AR-15 rifle, or how it feels to be without his heavy rucksack. I wonder, what is my father thinking as he poses near the Hao-Hiep sign?

Always away from home he poses with his friends: Parrish, Silvernail, Keen, Lindewold, Hallberg. Dead or alive, these men and more stay forever tucked away and remembered: Captain

Hubbard, Kim San, Dan the Cambodian interpreter, Sergeant Lopez, Garza, Matthews, Leon, Taylor. From their letters I find out that many referred to my father as a "soldier's soldier."

I discover from a telephone call that my father met one of his fellow soldiers, Bob Skyles, at church somewhere in the Third Corps of Vietnam. He and Skyles grew quickly attached to one another, so when someone from home sent my father a salt-cured ham in the mail, he shared it with him. A package of serrated knives arrived as well, and my father gave Skyles one of them. For six weeks while they were stationed south of Saigon, they talked in the evenings about the Blue Ridge Parkway that my father said he wanted to walk before he died. They didn't participate in the card games, movies, or drinking at the bar but instead talked for hours about what my father called "that pretty country" and how wonderful it would be to walk those mountains someday. Skyles described to me the large plywood sign in Saigon filled with the names of Special Forces guys who had been killed. "After awhile the sheet became filled and another one was put up next to it. It became depressing to drive by."

In this war of daily dead, I don't see my father's concerns on film. Later, his friend Edgell fills in the details for me. He tells me that at night at the compound my father would speak to Edgell or Captain Iacabelli about his worries. What do I do with this credit card bill from my wife? What do I do about my son's asthma? Should I be home? Pay the bill, Edgell tells him. Edgell remembers my father staring into a mirror hanging on the woven slat walls and pulling the skin on his neck taught. "Am I getting wrinkled?" he asked.

Edgell also tells me about the time he and my father borrowed a jeep from the captain and headed into Saigon to drink. They were in a hurry, he says, and didn't even take time to shower after having spent a week in the jungle. In one of the villages outside Bien Hoa, Edgell had a small accident with a Vietnamese bicyclist. MPs came running out of a store, jumped into their truck, and chased the borrowed jeep. Sirens went off and lights flashed. My father pulled out his pistol and shot five rounds into the MPs' truck radiator so that he and Edgell could get away. They cut across the field in the captain's jeep and then hid it behind a shed inside the Mike Force compound.

The photographs come to an end somewhere in the middle of my father's last album. The album is an inexpensive white scrapbook so different from his earlier leather albums with their special paper between the labeled pages. This one seems to have been bought on the run and the photographs quickly placed on the pages with no time for labeling.

My mind fills in again what was never photographed. It is always as if it were yesterday: I see a Ramsey policeman directing cars on New Street. After all these years, I still hear Aunt Edith and my father's cousin Dolly asking where to put the casseroles they brought. Where do you want the plates to go, Luella? My grandmother's house fills with people. Soldiers come from far away for this day: Higgenbotham, Edgell, Captain Iacabelli, Tally, Jan Janasac. Their class A uniforms are immaculate; their green berets with "De Oppresso Liber" written on them rest at the correct angle. Janasac's eyes fill with tears as he watches six-year-old Wesley fill his plate with food. Sergeant Higgenbotham keeps calling us "sweetie," and that more than anything else this day makes me want to cry. The echoes of a gun salute ring in all of our ears. That is the beginning of my forgetting. I slide back inside myself, enveloped in a private sadness I will not share for decades. Only my writing will someday pull out these memories.

Already five of my father's soldier friends have died during the time it has taken me to write this book. These are not the young soldiers who went to Vietnam but the older ones, many now in their seventies, from the original Special Forces group. If I want to see or hear from these guys, now is the time. They are dying from diseased hearts, war wounds, Agent Orange, and cancer. Very soon many who knew my father will take their memories to the grave.

I am the kind of person who stands in the theater aisle unable to leave until the credits roll by to the very end. I imagine there is a longer view of my father's friends than the one I've made contact with. It makes it difficult to leave this manuscript, as if I could give a final summary of my father's life. A wrap-up doesn't seem possible. I must wrap around his life like the material of one garment winding over the body of another garment.

Gift of a Liberated Village

When awards were given at the yearly convention of airborne associations in Atlanta, an artist who draws Medal of Honor recipients gave a drawing of my father to a man-of-the-year award winner named Stiles Thomas, a member of the Thirteenth Airborne Division Association. The drawing was to be given to the Silent Wings Airborne Museum in Tyrol, Texas. Mr. Thomas took one look at the drawing and exclaimed, "It's Charlie!" He and my father had gone to Ramsey High School together, and it was Thomas's father, Congressman J. Parnell Thomas, who was instrumental in petitioning the Canadian government to get my father out of the Canadian army on behalf of my grandparents and who had helped my father to pass his physical for entrance into the American army.

Stiles Thomas got in touch with my grandmother to get my sister Janice's address in order to tell her about the drawing's whereabouts. Janice had gone to high school in New Jersey with his daughter. In their correspondence, Janice sent him a poem about my father called "I Thought of You Today," which he read at the next Thirteenth Airborne Division reunion. "There wasn't a dry eye in the group," he told me on the phone.

When the citizens of La Motte, France, the first village liberated in southern France by the U.S. Airborne in 1944, presented the association with a sculptured plaque by the artist Pizay in 1991, the association decided to give the plaque to Janice. The round plaque shows a bust of a helmeted U.S. paratrooper looking up at the airplanes in the sky. La Motte is written right under a landing parachute. The drawing, Janice's poem, and soon the plaque will all reside at the Silent Wings Museum. Thomas wrote to the mayor of La Motte:

Mayor Yves Rose   Sept. 27, 1991
City Hall
Town of La Motte
Dept. of Var
France
Dear Mayor Rose:
On behalf of the men of the 13th Airborne Division, I would

like to thank you for the "Pizay" Plaque. Madame Sevestre presented it to us at our 10th annual reunion held in Niagara Falls, New York last week. We will soon be giving the plaque to the children of one of the men who parachuted into southern France with the 509th Parachute Infantry Battalion. This man was killed in action in Vietnam and was awarded the Congressional Medal of Honor for his heroism. Please convey to the citizens of La Motte our deep appreciation for the plaque.
With best regard.
Sincerely,
Stiles Thomas, Pres.
13th Airborne Division Association

Heaven's Dance Floor

f Heaven is all my mother said it was, then she's up there right now dancing with Elvis Presley. I believe she's smiling, maybe even laughing out loud as they rock and roll hand in hand over the dance floor. My father's watching from the sidelines, waiting his turn, ready to tell Elvis about my mother's collection of his records. Elvis smiles bashfully the way he did when he first began singing.

Both Elvis and my mother have lots to talk about: every single one of his movies my mother saw, the army, how they were both stationed in Germany at the same time. They are surprised at their similarities: how people grin at their southern accents, their Appalachian shyness. In their talk they find out just how far Germany is from the folks back home.

My mother discovers in Heaven that she's just as fine a person as she knows Elvis to be. She tells him that the best times of her life were dancing with her girlfriends to his music coming out of our prized German Rundpunkt record player. She describes how she and the other army wives pushed back the quartermaster-issued furniture and danced every afternoon as they fell in love with him over and over again.

She quotes his songs from memory: *Won't you wear my ring around your neck, Don't step on my blue suede shoes, It'll be a blue, blue Christmas without you.* When the music stops, they talk about their slow swirl into the abyss, and how even their families couldn't pull them out. If you didn't know who they were, from a distance you might think you were watching a country girl and a country boy remembering the death of someone they both knew.

Just as a tear comes to my mother's eyes, Elvis takes her hand and they start dancing again. There are no tears in Heaven; my mother once told me that. Elvis's hips gyrate now just like the night they did on *The Ed Sullivan Show*. My mother finds the rhythm of her own body again, tosses her head back in laughter, and moves out of memory onto Heaven's dance floor.

Anonymous

I often tease my husband that I want to dye my hair purple. I even bought a purple wig once and wore it for Halloween. To me it's the rebellion I never accomplished as a teenager; but more significantly it's a metaphor for wanting to be noticed, which might then lead to the possibility of finally being known.

Looking back, I think I've been anonymous my whole life. I have blended into the backdrop: a girl child on an army base in the days when only men were soldiers, surrounded by men identified by their uniform and military decorations. It was, as Mary Edwards Wertsch wrote in *Military Brats*, as if I were searching for my own reflection in a room without mirrors. The men saluted only each other and were aware of my presence only as a military dependent. They provided youth activities on base like bingo, swimming lessons, and camp, as if these would keep us out of the way. They gave us gifts at Christmas time when all the enlisted men and their families gathered at the mess hall for Christmas dinner. "Army dependent" said it all. They could function without us, but we couldn't without them.

Early on I watched how the women weren't allowed jobs. None of their overt opinions were tolerated. The women had each other, and that was their way of connection and meaning. They had a siblinglike closeness. They entered each other's small apartments for a cup of sugar, news from their real home, or hours of lonely talk when the men were away for extended time on maneuvers. Some sat anonymously in their apartments waiting for the tour of duty to be over or the chance to move back to the States.

Some women came to life with their husbands on weekends at the enlisted men's club. It was a time for dancing as a couple and always lots of drinking; a time to feel that they belonged, that they were a part of something bigger than their army-issued home. Sometimes the men wore civilian suits on those weekend occasions, giving life a sense of normal activity.

My mother never drank in her early years of marriage. She was young, unworldly, and naive, having never left her poor farm beginnings before life with my father. Little by little she gave in to the drinking that was so much a part of army culture. I see now it was her way of giving in to the crowd, of fighting back with my father, of wanting to belong. The parties at "the club" relieved her lonely anonymous feeling and connected her to the army world. It was her ultimate mask for all the denial, secrecy, classified information, stoicism, and off-limits parts of being an army wife – all "standard issue: the basic equipment without which the mission cannot be accomplished."

I knew early on that part of the military mission was the American flag. But except for saluting the flag, which I did at school and at five o'clock retreat every day, I wasn't sure what being an American was. In an odd way, I was purged of that place called America because I lived removed from its mass. I learned about U.S. history while surrounded by bombed-out buildings still standing from the Second World War. I read about the Vermont Mountain Boys, Amelia Earhart, and Dolly Madison as I walked among strangers who spoke another language. The German children thought they knew me – winner of The War, a rich American, but I was neither. I was anonymous both to my country and to the foreign country in which I lived. My mother, who felt American through and through, was lonely in this world of anonymity.

When I left Europe in 1963 for the United States, I entered the civilian world for the first time. My parents separated, my father remained on base in Germany, my mother went to live with her parents in Illinois, and I went to live with my father's mother in New Jersey just thirty-five miles outside New York City. Suddenly I stopped seeing soldiers as crossing guards and keepers of the fortress. I stopped needing my dog tags for identification. I was no longer labeled an army brat. I had to rewrite my personal script to fit in.

I tried hard to blend into the crowd and never spoke of my father's parachute jumps for extra pay, maneuvers in the dead of winter, or Radio Free Europe. I was afraid my description of the hollowed-out mortar shells my father used as bookends for his blue army manuals would turn off my civilian friends. Nowhere did I see in someone else's living room olive drab shells with things like USMA 1954, 60 MM printed on the smooth sides. I knew the shell's musty smell of old firings would separate my friends' world from mine even farther.

Ironically, the town I moved into had been named after my ancestors, the Ramseys from Scotland, who first settled in these parts in the eighteenth century. I had no idea about that then. I never knew then that my father's great-grandmother Mary Sophia Ramsey was the daughter of William James Ramsey, called "Whiskey Bill" by many. He had been a hotel and tavern owner up on the Franklin Turnpike, I now know. His father, James William Ramsey, was killed driving a horse in New York City. The Ramseys married Blauvelts, who married Fishers, who married a Bartholf, who married a Hosking. All of them had settled on this New Jersey soil long before I arrived.

I was moving through this land of theirs, tiptoeing from the military to the civilian. How to explain the army to my civilian friends? How to talk about my parents' separation when I had no idea of its meaning myself? How to live now as a granddaughter rather than a daughter? The girls at my new school already wore stockings, had learned social dancing, and talked about lipsticks. I had just come from the protected environment of guarded gates, still wore anklets, and played with dolls. My anonymity came from being a stranger among those who had known each other all their lives. A stranger among those who had no real clue what the cold war meant. At the time of life when all I wanted was to be like my friends, I felt as if I belonged nowhere. This typical adolescent feeling was probably not unique, but it was to shape and remain with the woman I became.

Before I had time to feel at home, my father returned from Europe in the summer of 1963 and within six months took his first tour of duty in Vietnam. I buried this part of my life and revealed it to no one. It was a difficult time to be the daughter of a warrior. How could I hold on to loyalty when those around me had lost theirs? How could I explain to the civilians of my new school off the Fort Bragg base about a father going to war when the whole country wasn't involved in this war? Was it maneuvers or a real war? I didn't really know then. Men can die in either.

As the talk of Vietnam escalated on television, I numbed out, didn't pay attention to what I saw, pretended I never heard it. It was like staring at something intensely but never ever really seeing it. I spent all my teenage years that way. I was there, and I wasn't there. Finally, I became anonymous even to myself.

In college in upstate New York in 1968, the year after my father's death in Vietnam, I began paying attention to the Vietnam War protests for the first time. In the midst of this, I was invited to the White House in the spring of 1969 with my family to watch my six-year-old brother receive my father's Congressional Medal of Honor. Before I went, I had to ask a professor for permission to reschedule a history exam. Only when I realized he was annoyed with me did I tell him why I was going to Washington, D.C. He raised his eyebrows with a look of shock on his face. Whether it was a look of respect or disgust, I never found out and wouldn't, at the time, begin to ask him. I added his look to the silence I carried.

My boyfriend, Bruce, who would someday become my husband, drove me in his dark green MG Midget to the airport, which was an hour away from campus. There we were looking like the tiniest piece of America, a college couple driving out of the village of Alfred toward Rochester. But there was a gigantic split between us. Here was a true civilian, a protesting seventies student who made fun of his then-mandatory ROTC uniform, driving his military brat girlfriend to the airport for a ceremony with Nixon at the White House. Silence and tension filled the car in a mixture of controversy, pride, and confusion. All we knew in those moments was that we loved each other and hoped that love could transcend what the country couldn't.

I left and returned and never spoke to anyone about the medal. Even in my hazy vision, I knew it was not a welcome topic. I didn't want to be identified with the army or Vietnam. Nor was I a protester. I was caught between two poles. I blanked out as if the language around me was foreign, as if I were two separate people who never met each other. I was divided from myself, the protesters, and the soldiers, much the way my country was divided about the war itself. The only thing I knew was that the warriors were not faceless or inhuman.

For those who thought they knew me, it looked as if I belonged. I was an active student moving in and out of a variety of friendships: Jews from Long Island, Polish Catholics from Buffalo, upstate farmers, South Americans. Graduate school at Iowa State University, teaching first grade, and my early years of marriage came and went. The silence remained. On occasion in the right atmosphere, I would mention my father's military connection, like the time an ex–navy commander turned school principal hired me for a kindergarten teacher's position. When he said he ran the school like a battleship, I mentioned my father.

Mostly I remember dinner parties where I sat at the table anonymous to everyone there while they spoke about the sixties, growing up in the civilian world, and how they were lucky enough to get out of the Vietnam War. My silence assured everyone I was just like them – that our lives had been the same. "Remember those high school pool parties?" a friend asked. I wanted to tell her about the twelve schools I attended, the housing project where I lived once while my father was away, my grandmothers' old homes, the war. I wanted to describe life in the fortress, but I never knew where to begin. I became a social chameleon instead.

It was this identified sense of anonymity that brought me to writing letters for Amnesty International prisoners of conscience. The thought of someone unknown who had been put in a cell for no other reason than speaking his or her mind brought me to the typewriter over and over again. I pictured my father captured somewhere without anyone knowing – how thankful I'd be if someone would have written a letter to let an official know. How imprisoned within myself I often felt – desperate for words.

When our first son was still an infant and sleeping one rainy afternoon in our third-floor apartment, I took the framed eight-by-ten photograph of my father in uniform out of my drawer and placed it on my living room shelf. I said nothing as I reached into my husband's childhood dresser and pulled out what I had hidden for years. It had always felt to me as if my father's presence and his uniform would not be tolerated by anyone who entered my home. It never occurred to me before to begin the process of breaking the silence. I was deeply afraid it would remind me of that gap I had felt once in my husband's car. What it was that made me bring it out that afternoon I can't remember. Perhaps it was my sleeping son — his past, his future — that gave me the courage. As it rained outside, I felt the beginnings of something I couldn't explain. After years of secrecy, I was surprised at my sudden boldness but not at my anxious stirrings.

A couple of years later, when I was four months pregnant with my second child, I went to the Vietnam Memorial Wall with my husband and three-year-old son. It was the first time I allowed myself the public affirmation of having been part of that war, of having lost someone irreplaceable. I had not expected to feel anything at this wall everyone was talking about because I had grown accustomed to the walls around my heart. But when I saw my father's name and my family's reflection in the black stone, I stood there with tears flowing down my face. My heart was inescapably heavy; my throat choked with all the words I had never spoken. I found myself for the first time wanting to talk to those who surrounded me. Who did you lose? What was his name? Tell me your story, I wanted to say. My husband found a ladder, and I climbed it to touch my father's name and had my son do the same. It was as if my three-year-old son, the son not born yet, and my husband were actually meeting my father, and I was beginning the long process of giving birth to my past. I wonder if that moment at the memorial didn't pass into the son I was carrying and have something to do with his infant fretfulness, his inconsolableness.

I came to my father's photograph collection at much the same time our country opened up to the subject of Vietnam. When protesters could sit at the same table with daughters of warriors and talk about their differences and recognize their similarities, then and only then could I begin. I began observing each of my father's photographs for only the surface, much like I had looked at the whole war. Slowly I stepped thin layer by thin layer through the photographs. With each stratum I allowed myself what I had never done before. I put into words what I had been carrying around for years. And with that I became known to myself, built from the ground up.

French troops, 1954.

Indochine

n 1966 a French writer named Bernard B. Fall wrote a book called *Hell in a Very Small Place* about the siege of Vietnam's Dien Bien Phu. In the years my family was in Europe surrounded by the silent warriors of the cold war, Fall was in Vietnam accompanying French Union Forces and researching behind Communist lines. In those days I would have thought hell in a very small place boiled down to the lives of some friends whose apartments smelled like urine-soaked diapers. But places would not have been part of my vocabulary then. While I focused on a narrow portion of this earth, one of the decisive battles of the twentieth century was taking place between the French and the Vietminh. My life was to be shaped by that event during the spring of 1954. The ninth anniversary of V-E Day, the victory of the Allies over Nazi Germany, became the anniversary of the French defeat and the American government turning its head even closer toward the east. As one U.S. officer later told Fall, "What we are doing here basically is we're exorcising Dien Bien Phu."

By the time Fall's book was published, my father was already in Vietnam and just around the corner from his death. Fall wrote that it was more important than ever not to succumb to the temptation to throw in our lot with those who view Vietnam in simple terms of grand strategy, Chinese aggression, or American lust for power, no matter how difficult the trail of truth and how heavy the burden of the record.

Twenty-seven years after my father's death in Vietnam, I go to a movie about the French involvement in Vietnam up to the Geneva Convention. From the beginning, I found it difficult to tell where I began and the movie, *Indochine*, left off. Afterward I couldn't respond when someone asked, "Wasn't the movie beautiful?" I felt that old familiar wedge of space between me and my civilian friends.

I was tense throughout most of the film; my jaw muscles gripped tightly as I watched. It was as if it were *me* escaping to the north, *my* life that contained such dangers. The violence left me fearful; I imagined the peace I lived in now invaded and destroyed like the fragile peace of the Bay of Haiphong. I was inside the film and I was not. I was a coolie, a Communist, a soldier, a sailor, a sedated opium user. It was then and it was now. I was French, Vietnamese, and American — all this and no one at the same time.

I walked out of the theater as defended as I had walked in. During and after the film I felt outside myself, as if watching from elsewhere. When a friend I had come with asked me if the film was painful because of my father's time in Vietnam, I didn't answer. I felt that words would fail me and that to say yes would have simplified it, making it a predictable final response. In the cold, breathless night as we walked back to the car over layers of hardened snow, I couldn't give any answer.

After I dropped her off and her porch light had gone out, I burst into tears. I cried as if having just come from the funeral of someone I couldn't live without. Suddenly I saw my father on a long chain of historical events that created what we now know as Vietnam. I magnified what I imagined he saw in his three tours of duty there. His death was only a piece of Vietnam, a piece so small even a microscope lens wouldn't be able to find it. It was this insignificance that brought me to tears.

Back at home at my desk I looked at my father's photographs of Vietnam and saw an old Buddhist temple with French troops lined up outside and the date 1954 on the back. I saw that the ghosts of rubber trees, so clear in the movie, came alive as well in my father's pictures. He photographed rows and rows of skinny, silver rubber trees that looked like they were in perpetual moonlight. Jeeps and guns and silence and sunlight weren't left out of his photographs. He only left out parts of Vietnam's history: coolies in pointed straw hats, French buckets that held the drips pouring slowly from each tree year after year, Dien Bien Phu. His photographs didn't speak the French he learned before he left America's shore. What echoed through his endless rows of rubber trees I stared at was Vietnam's silent witness.

As I drifted off to sleep in my own bed, I remembered the love between a man and a woman in the movie. Yes, that was beautiful. A bay with ancient jutting edges lifting up from inside the earth. Yes, that too. But it was difficult for me to appreciate the beauty of *Indochine*. As its art bled into my real life, it was as if I were noticing drops of blood falling one by one into buckets alongside the rubber trees. As if I saw night spreading over the abandoned plantations and eyes with cocked rifles appearing out of nowhere. As if I were hearing again stories of a soldier waking up inside his tent to find his buddy beheaded, ears of prisoners cut off for souvenirs, babies napalmed, rice fields exploded, villages burned. All I could think of were those lonely men and women watching their futures shatter with one step forward into a hot, booby-trapped jungle.

Still, the trees of my father's photographs reflect the moon's light. The lines between art and life melt into a background of lush green and haunting red blood. *Indochine* is a world gone mad, a beauty turned inside out. The past finds its way into my present life, where I often have no words.

Dispatches

Sometimes when I read books about the Vietnam War, or "Vietnam Conflict," as one administrator from Fort Bragg kept referring to it on the phone with me, I walk around stunned for days as if I'm not sure what world I'm in anymore. Some books like Michael Herr's *Dispatches* leave me so shaky I'm afraid to pick up the book after I've put it down, as if it's a grenade that could detonate in my face any minute. I pick fights with my husband and feel like walking for miles, wondering just what it is I'm running from. I don't make my bed, thinking I might need to crawl back in again before the day is over. I can't eat breakfast alone in my house after everyone's left for school or work. I walk around the house instead, wrapping my arms around my body, crying, not sure about what, but crying like a little girl who's lost somewhere, feeling so absolutely lonely she might die on the spot. Suddenly I don't know a soul I could phone for help.

I recall a phrase used by this same administrator/historian/archivist when I called him to see if there was anything there in the files from my father — any leftover action reports he wrote or any Special Forces information lying around that I might copy for my research. I wanted contact with my father, wanted to see what it was he saw. I wanted to be in the field with him. The archivist was polite and tried to be helpful but then said that if I had known the army in the 1970s I would know why they wanted to get rid of all that stuff — why tons of records were shredded and what remained, if anything, was sent up to the National Archives in Washington, D.C. "I guess you could call it 'forced amnesia,'" he said.

After that phone call I walked around the rest of the day saying "forced amnesia" over and over again, out loud, just to hear what it sounded like. I thought if I could memorize its sound I could allow myself to believe that what my father had fought for had been shredded, as if in doing so this country could move on to the next conflict, move on before it looked too closely or asked too many questions of its higher ups. I thought of how violent "forced" sounded to me. I had believed just like my friend who suggested I make the call that the reports would actually be there. We are still believers. But the phone call reminded me that we are a nation that is forgetting. We are no different now than in the Civil War, when Walt Whitman wrote that the real war would never get into the books. Perhaps that is the nature of war itself.

I had thought that the archivist could have helped me, could have made my job easier. But it is clear to me now that this stranger could give me nothing except the concern in his voice or his wishing me well. My job became sharply defined the more I thought about it. I would remember what this country wants to forget. Making this book is a counterattack to the shredding. I am back in the field putting together my father's mutilated body, limb by limb, remembering what was once dismembered. I am removing the masks of secrecy, stoicism, and denial I learned as an army brat. I am offsetting this forced amnesia.

I am filled to overflowing with images in the books about the Vietnam War I keep picking up at the library, images of fields of dead bodies, shells that explode into a pile of full body bags and leave a mess no one wants to clean up — "a real shit detail," Herr wrote. I see images of soldiers carrying around things like five-pound Bibles or a cookie from home as good luck charms, or a doctor refusing to treat wounded Vietnamese soldiers because he said he took the Hippocratic oath in America. Sometimes I think I can't bear one more image of a lit cigarette in a jungle just to keep the mosquitoes from swarming into someone's mouth. But still I read the books and look at their pictures, maybe hoping to find my father on one of the pages. Maybe I believe he'll come to life for me through someone else's words.

But each time I read I think I don't want to see my father on those pages. I don't want to feel anyone else's insanity — the "we're here to kill gooks" or the "if it ain't the fucking incoming, it's the fucking outgoing," writers like Herr hear in Vietnam. Each time I am confronted with these images, I pass through the child I was, the young woman caught in a web of loss, and the woman for whom I am searching now between the dearth of material from the government and the density of material from other writers. I decide that it is these images that I must absorb, that I can't let them have the same effect on me as a writer that the government had on us as a people.

I realize, with each book I force myself to read, that what I've been doing with my father's photographs is plunging into the war again and again, making contact, walking over contorted bodies I never saw, listening for the "motherfucker, shit, big deal" language of soldiers I never met. I have been filling in the gaps surrounding my father, reminding myself that there is a family for each one of those bodies zipped into a black rubber bag.

I pick up another book, another title and turn the pages one by one until, for a few moments, I am there feeling the war in all its fire-fighting fear and I'm scared out of the mind I know I would lose if I were really there. I am in an agitated half-sleep going through the day's schedule. Images drift in and out of my head, the sky looks strangely surreal, my eyes burn, and my heart can barely contain its beatings.

A friend calls me while I'm reading Herr's *Dispatches* and I think I will try to tell her about it, but I can't suddenly find any words. I tell her that I've just picked a fight with my husband and that this book I'm reading is blowing me away. She reminds me that it's easier to get angry with my husband than to understand where my real anger lies. I think to myself, what is it I'm angry at? I say to her that maybe I'm angry at the whole country and that just feels too big to take on. I think as I say it that maybe she feels like I've drawn a line between myself and the rest of the country and she's in that other part. I know that's not true — nothing, not one single thing in life is that simple. Then just what does a daughter of a dead warrior do all these years later? What does she say? Where does she put all these images? How does she find peace, and I don't mean just the absence of war.

The warrior's daughter grows up to write what it means to be just that. She writes to find her own identity, to retaliate against the dismembering of her father, to offset the forgetting. She writes to recreate life again, to remove one of those body bags from the mass. She knows that only a writer can answer some questions and that she will find her father on the pages she writes.

In bringing my father back to life, I am bringing them all back into our sight. I am finding my father's spirit that will not be crushed, like the snake coiled up on the early American colonial flag that Finvola writes me about. I enter the field of writing like my father entered his life, highly conscious of what he was doing. She reminds me that he knew he couldn't always count on relief in the fields, that he had to use what he had available. He accepted his vocation with the courage I reach inside to find now. He reengaged with the action over and over again the way I must do in my writing.

May 12, 1995

oday is my father's birthday. He would have been seventy-one years old. How to transform someone frozen in time into the look he would have, if only? Would he have lost his hair? Turned gray? Would I recognize him? Sometimes I find myself looking at men in their seventies and trying to make the giant leap from forty-two to seventy-one.

At other times I find myself meeting my father when I least expect it. Recently at Verzuvios Restaurant, two Italian men sang and played Italian songs with a mandolin and guitar in front of our table. In the melodic foreign words of "Arrivederci Roma" and "Luna Rosa" I felt as if my father, who was not Italian or had any Italian ancestors but who loved the music of Europe, had just walked in the room. It was language foreign to my father's ears that he loved, played on our radio, or used with my sisters and me around daily domestic things like coming to dinner or brushing our teeth. He sang French, German, or Italian songs when he was happy. He spoke Czech whenever he found someone who understood.

Hearing the music reminded me of him as a young paratrooper in Naples, or the time he was found in Spain laughing in a bar filled with Spaniards. I imagined him singing "Prosit" with a perfect accent in a German *Gasthaus* or speaking to villagers in Vietnam. He was lost in the sound of language as if touched by its rhythms, as if each strange phrase was a piece of the puzzle my father was. The music of these two Italian strangers filled my eyes with sudden tears.

A man named Tom Connolly who had read a piece about my father I wrote for the newspaper called me in the days leading up to my father's birthday. He too had been in the Battle of the Bulge when he was eighteen. He too had spent cold days and nights fighting the Germans. He said that he and a comrade had taken a young soldier who could have been my father off the battlefield. The wounded soldier's name was "Snake." "There just can't be that many people named Snake," he said. "And in the same battle!"

After meeting with Mr. Connolly and looking over his memorabilia about the Second World War, I remembered my father had been wounded the day after Christmas and not in January, when Mr. Connolly remembered carrying "Snake" off the snow-covered field. And I remembered my father didn't acquire the nickname "Snake" until after the war. "It would have been a wonderful co-incidence, a great story," I tell him.

He explains the World War II Victory Medal, the Armed Forces Expeditionary Medal, and the American Campaign Medal to me. He tells me about the planes of the 1940s – how twelve para-troopers like my father flew in these planes with no seats, only benches along the side. A steel cable, he says, ran across the plane from the tail to the pilot and was called the static line, like the title of an airborne newspaper I receive. Young men would hook up to this cable while waiting for their turn to jump, sometimes singing: "Gory, gory, what a hell of a way to die!"

I am interested in Mr. Connolly's photographs, his newspaper clippings, and his Dwight D. Eisenhower book, *The Crusade in Europe*. But mostly I am intrigued by his face. I keep staring at him as if searching for the younger soldier within. I look at what seventy-one looks like over and over again, thinking for a few seconds I am in the same room as my father.

Voice

I envy the details I read of other authors who write about their fathers because I have to work so hard to come up with those that I do remember. It seems these other writers are able to construct a timeline, a continuous story with a beginning, a middle, and an end. My writing is made up of pieces like my fa-ther's photograph collection. The images that I have start and stop like photos thrown in a scrapbook. How difficult to recall the years when my father left for war and no longer kept us together with his constant picture taking. Now I weave back and forth through time, never straight forward, always trying to bring the past into the present, always trying to sidestep the death I know is coming.

I hear myself say that my memory is a blur, as if my past flew by me in one big shadow and I couldn't stop time to memorize its de-tails. My remembering cannot be recalled at will. Sometimes I think I lack authority over my memory. Like the returning vets Jonathan Shay writes about in his book *Achilles in Vietnam*, my memory is not a complete narrative but more like a sensory replay of disconnected fragments. Like these vets, I am trying to create a language for that which was once silent. I am trying to get beyond the persistence of numbing — a basic survival skill — and into the world of listening, remembering, and grieving.

Years after the war, I am finally finding the time and safety to mourn — a process that was once built into ancient Greek warfare but never into the Vietnam War. By writing I am saying that the survivor cannot be silenced. I am breaking the aloneness and finding language for my father's life in his world, where words meant nothing and only action counted. My father is one of the unanchored dead, restless like an unhealed wound. I see now that I have been one of the unanchored survivors, imprisoned in silence and obstructed grief.

As I come out of that silence, I begin to hear the voices of others. Larry Allen, a Korean War veteran and the evening security guard at city hall where I hung the photo/essay exhibition *Snake's Daughter*, stares reverently at my father's photographs as if looking for something. "You know, I've got a box of photographs from the war," he says to me finally. "I keep them under my bed. I ought to bring them out. I've never talked about the war before." Each time I come to check on the exhibit, he shows me more of the photographs he brings out of the box. He begins to put words to his eighteen-year-old war experience as if in my memorializing my father I gave him permission to speak.

Hugh Gordon, a retired Special Forces soldier and a one-time neighbor in Germany, wrote me that my interest in my father had inspired him to write his life. "I started when I was born and have gotten to my experience with the 82nd Airborne in the Battle of the Bulge," he said. "It's in my handwriting, and when I finish it will be my gift to my grandson and granddaughter. I write a little everyday and still have a long way to go."

I hear the voice over the phone of my father's company commander, a man named Frank Iacabelli, who recognizes the name Hosking immediately when his wife hands him the phone. "Oh my God," he says over and over again, and then I hear him take a deep breath like he's making room for the past to suddenly enter his life again. He tells me some of the things I have already heard: my father's perfect balance of caution and courage ("exactly what you'd want from a soldier"), his patriotism ("unusual for his time"), and his ambiguous feelings of where his ultimate duty lay ("country or family"). He tells me that he helped write my father's Medal of Honor citation and that he first met me at my father's funeral in New Jersey. I have no memory of that.

"Whenever I tell war stories, I talk about you and your sisters," Iacabelli tells me over the phone. "I will never forget meeting you. Your father talked in Vietnam about how proud he was of you guys, but I realized why when I walked into your grandmother's house and saw all of you standing there. That image of four beautiful children has remained with me."

I had not thought of myself as a war story; but this ex-soldier, this man who tells me when I ask if my father had been a replacement in the Mike Force that "nobody can be replaced," knows that war stories include more than just crazy bayonet charges or courage in a faraway jungle. They include as well the lives of children an ocean away. There are many voices in war.

I get off the phone and recognize how daughter's voice and vet's voice travel back and forth as if down a long tube that becomes progressively shorter and shorter and brings the war out of its hidden recesses. Maybe it is the way this Captain Iacabelli, this Mr. Iacabelli, this Frank says thank *you* when I give him thanks for his willingness to speak. Maybe it's the tenderness in his voice or the way I hear that he could go on for hours talking about a war he rarely speaks about anymore. Maybe it's the hunger I hear in both of our voices: hunger to speak, to recognize, and to honor.

Sometimes I feel as if I've been to war along with these soldiers I've come to know in my search for my father. I carry no visible war wounds; I am a woman, and it has been said by the ignorant that women do not know war. But it is these soldier-friends who know better. They help me break my "Medal of Honor silence" and give me stories to add to my father's photographs. They bring back the details of my father's life and anchor me to a time I once chose to forget. Their voices know what Homer knew so long ago, that telling stories is a healing art.

Another voice, the civilian voice of my writing friend, Finvola, travels these memories with me. She reminds me that my father "disappeared into action and that his action made the crucial difference." She points out that my writing is my action, my crucial difference. It is my way to find a voice. I will not let silence be the final killer, I tell her. I will not let my children, like tiny ants on a trail of sugar, carry that silence into their future. I will become what she calls me — "my father's writer." I will become my father's daughter again — Snake's daughter. I will let my voice rise along with all the others.

The Ultimate Mask

Through his photographs, my father has left some kind of substitute for his life, taken away by war. With these pictures, he reaffirms our family, allows us to see what he can no longer say, and gives us the details of his public life. But, as a writer, sometimes I have felt as Roland Barthes did when he was searching through photographs to find the essence of his mother. I strain toward who my father really was each time I confront one of his photographs as if I am climbing up a steep cliff. I feel sometimes as Barthe did, like I've climbed back down without having really seen him, only to begin all over again. My father preserves his existence, and at the same time the images he gave us immediately produce death because there is no future in the photographs. Left as they are, this ending is their ultimate suffering, the ultimate mask of my father's life.

But when I discover some small fragment within the photograph that touches me, I begin to enter that life. If I bring a part of myself into his life, I discover him. I am learning that it is not a polite study. I have to pound against the visual silence over and over again, to endure the tension of the encounters, and to open myself where I have been closed before. I have to find that small and complicated space that lies somewhere between the objective glance and the excruciating pain of the subjective and be willing to discover both our lives.

Out of the blue, my father's friend Peter Sheerin writes me from North Carolina: "Please Honey, continue your research on Snake. He was a true hero and a fearless combat leader. I hope you end up publishing something. It would represent all of us —

dead, crippled and alive. Get the truth and tell it the way it was." He offers to edit any manuscript I produce.

Angels have arrived on my doorstep each time I feel like stopping. Descriptions from my father's soldier friends reanimate the figure in the photographs. Bill Ramsdell writes me that my father's trademark was a frozen smile when they drank together at the NCO Club, that my father's civilian dress sometimes reminded him of Charlie Chaplin, and that he was called that by those who knew him intimately. Habitually, he carried a firing bolt of some alien weapon in his pocket and would challenge anyone to disassemble and reassemble it. I go back to the photographs with this knowledge and take a fresh look. Like my father had to do over and over again with his weapons, I am reassembling the parts of my father's life. I write to thank Ramsdell, and he writes back: "He who spends time with death will live in memoriam."

I ponder this soldier's honest expression, a cliché that holds truth in it, his authority to use such words. But it brings me up short. Is it death that I am living with, or is it life that I seek in my search? Does the writing itself keep me from the edges of chaos? Am I working against the limits, pursuing meaninglessness until I force it to mean something? Am I opening myself to my father's life, his death, only to look at my own life, my own death?

Late at night, looking over a Special Forces Monthly Operational Summary given to me by Jim Donahue, I gather more details. I read that in March 1967 two bridges were repaired in the area where my father was, 206 VC were killed, and 2,830,650 leaflets were disseminated. I hear from Donahue that the standards of the Special Forces were dropped at one point in the war because incoming troops couldn't be replaced and trained fast enough. The poorly trained soldiers were not able to withstand the rigors of isolation or the perilous life, nor did they have the independence required to live in the jungle without supplies for weeks at a time. There was too much preoccupation, he says, with the statistics of body counts and not enough of my father's knowledge of indigenous customs and language.

I read that a Mike Force team departed from Cau Song Be in Binh Long Province in an attempt to locate enemy units suspected of moving through the area. "Operations" were conducted, the summary says. As a result, one U.S. Special Forces soldier was killed, another one wounded, and one VC killed. The Mike Force company moved back to headquarters at Bien Hoa the next day, March 22, 1967. Death sweeps down and writes itself across the page. I pause with a silence that freezes me. There it is, that statistic, that one small figure in front of me: the one Special Forces soldier is my father.

I reach for a map and start to look for the Third Corps, where my father spent most of the war. There is the Song Be River. There is Bien Hoa — where is the sign, the wooden curved sign I came across seemingly by chance years ago in a Time-Life series called *This Fabulous Century?* I was waiting for my husband to finish his research at the Idaho State University library and reached over to touch the books on the shelf next to me. The pages fell open to a large color photograph of a place not on the map I look at now: "Camp Charles E. (Snake) Hosking, Co. A 5th Special Forces Group, Vietnam, Bien Hoa." The caption at the bottom of the picture read: "Green Berets fall in at their home base, looking, as a current ballad about them put it, like men who mean just what they say." I remember thinking as the sun came through the windows behind me that there must be 25,000 books in the library. Little did I know I was beginning my research about my father that day with this Hermeon gift. Returning to the photographs and the Bien Hoa dot on the map, I can't turn the pages quickly. The place once bore his name, my name. It can never again be a casual glance for me, an unknown place on a map.

My father writes from Bien Hoa to Sergeant Higgenbotham at Fort Bragg. Betty Higgenbotham sends me the yellowed letter she found in the attic after her husband's death. There had been a fire, and my father had lost everything he owned — two cameras, some pearls he was planning to send my mother, photographs, some money, weapons, and a radio. He wrote that he wanted to get his clothes ready for traveling home and needed the Special Forces chevrons for his uniform. They were out of them at the PX. "I'll be at Bragg in June and I'll pay you. I expect to be in the field quite a lot until then. I've got to get shaped up." He signs it "Chuck."

The cameras, the photographs, my father's urgent need to capture on film all that he was seeing — all up in smoke. How is it that so many photographs survived his perilous life? Again in this letter I find my father's unwavering attention to detail. Already in April he is planning for the exact uniform he will need to travel home. The ways of the seasoned soldier, the regulations he follows to the letter — again revealed. I go back to the albums and wonder just what else was destroyed by fire a year before his death. What images am I missing? What details are still hidden?

Not all the facts of my father's life in Vietnam were lost on the men my father called the enemy. I read in Ray Bows's book *Vietnam: Military Lore 1959–1973* that by 1965 my father's zeal and aggressiveness in fighting became known to the Vietcong, who placed a bounty on his head. During one particular mortar attack on his camp, they demanded over a loudspeaker that my father be handed over to them, or else. His name was placed on their list of most wanted men. Now it is I, all these years later, who hunts for my father, sending out messages: where is he, how do I find him?

My father sports a Vietcong helmet and rubber sandals in one of the photographs in Bows's book. He kneels before a cache of equipment captured in "a sweep through the rubber trees." His tattooed left bicep faces the camera, and I strain to remember the image's distinctive blue shape. I bring out my magnifying glass and see it might be an eagle on his arm — a bird ready to fly away. I follow the photograph down to his toes and stare at them, wondering if as a child I ever really did look at them. I remember his feet were forever in big, black polished boots. Those were the feet I remember, not the naked toes. The big toe on his right foot suddenly looks just like mine. I bring the magnifying glass up to his eyes and think for a moment he is staring right into my eyes as if he always knew I'd finally be looking. His delicate features are strong and confident. He looks like he is sure he is where he should be.

Reading further, I find my father leaning up against his rucksack under some trees near the Saigon River in the Binh Duong Province. The writing underneath the picture says it is his fourth day out. His rifle lies behind him, his canteen to his right, his arms folded against his stomach, his knees bent, his feet inside jungle boots resting on something I can't see. He appears to be asleep, a rare moment for my father, who never seemed to need much sleep. Another look and I notice that his hair has grown longer in his absence from home. It was something my mother had often wished for, perhaps because it made it less "regulation army" and more the man she wanted to spend time with. The blond hair combs back the way I see it in his adolescent photographs, but now there is a receding hairline along the edges, just like the one my beautician pointed out to me as I sat in a chair before the mirror.

Bows writes of search-and-destroy missions, of gathering information on enemy lines of communication. He writes of an operation in which my father flanked the enemy, killing seven insurgents, causing the remainder to withdraw so that a comrade wounded in the stomach could be carried from the killing zone. He cites the Bronze Star my father received for that action, adding that my father and his patrols crossed into Cambodia on a regular basis to accomplish their missions. This can be written and believed finally after all these years when Nixon denied we were ever in Cambodia. How is it that I remember knowing it then? Had my father told me once, knowing someday it would mean something serious to me? Sometimes the line between what I remember and what I read in books and see in photographs is blurred like permanent ghosts.

I think back to my father's longtime friend, Sergeant Laudacina, and recall instantly their laughing together doing a dance they made up in our small living room in Fayetteville. Earlier that evening, my father had filched some bricks from a builder down the street so he could make a bookshelf in our living room. Laudacina, as my parents called him, knew about my father's plan and phoned, pretending he was a police officer who knew about the bricks. My father was visibly frightened, as if he had just been caught in the act. I remember his anxious pacing back and forth down the hall between the living room and my parents' bedroom. Later, when Laudacina came over and revealed the joke, they began dancing and clapping their hands as they bent over in laughter with each shuffle step. That scene remains in my memory, a reminder of my father's playfulness, his risk taking, and his capacity for fear. It tells me of his childlike shame of getting caught, losing stripes, and falling short of his high standards.

When they both went to Vietnam, Laudacina as a career counselor and my father with the Mike Force, my mother and Mrs. Laudacina spent a lot of time together in her trailer park. Years later, after both my father's and Laudacina's deaths, my sister Betty Ann called her, hoping to visit while passing through Fayetteville. Mrs. Laudacina barely spoke on the other end, as though she had forgotten all those hours we had played in the back rooms of her trailer while she and my mother spoke of war and the daily details of life at home. She didn't invite my sister over, and Betty Ann felt erased from her life. She hung up the phone feeling unsettled, as if Mrs. Laudacina blamed her for the deaths.

In my father's letter of February 1966, he writes that "Sgt. Laudacina should arrive in country on 28 of February. He will be assigned to AG Admin Co. USARV as a recruiter in Saigon." He added, "I'll be glad to get back to Bien Hoa. I'm tired of rice, fish, etc. and will be glad to have eggs and bacon for breakfast. We eat twice a day here. Cold rice in the field and dried fish or mutton. The water tastes like iodine because you have to put so many tablets in it since we drink from the canals or paddies. When we are in from operations I boil the water for hot tea. I laugh when I hear over the radio to avoid malaria – sleep with mosquito nets and stay out of mosquito infested areas. Incidentally I have a seven transistor three band National radio, present of the VC which I got the other day."

In this letter from the field – in the language of my father, the linguist – the structure is sometimes awkward, words are crossed out, some sentences are mere fragments. It's as if he's jumping from safety at Bien Hoa to the memory of home and back to the reality of the field. He writes from the Mekong Delta, near a canal called Kinh Gay Kinh Tra Cu, which flows out of Cambodia. He tells us about the death of one USSF soldier and the evacuation to the United States of another one wounded in action. Then in the same letter, just lines away from death, he hopes we are all doing well in school, that he is worried about my mother because he knows we "love her so much."

There is something revealed in that statement about my mother, I think suddenly as I read it again. It's as though he can't be sure of his position away from home if he can't be sure of hers. It comes to me across time with my father's language. I look at the date at the top of the letter, February 1966, and think back to that year. My father must have known by then that my mother was six months pregnant with the child of another man, a man none of us ever met. By now my mother had written my father several times in code, trying hard to tell him what she could barely write down on the page. How do I know this? Did I find that letter in her hot apartment after her death, still folded in her drawer, yellowed with age? The one she found in his olive drab trunk returned from Vietnam? And where is it now as I search my house for those things I brought back after her funeral?

Nowhere in my father's photographs do I see the entire warp and weft of my parents' marriage. Nowhere do his albums show the decline of my mother as the war declined. The personal cost to people's lives. His leaving, his coming, his leaving again. His return from Vietnam after my sister Joy was born. My mother taking Joy to her sister's house during my father's visit so he wouldn't have to see her. The way my father slipped into my mother's bed at that reunion as if he had never left, as if what they had together had not been lost, as if the war was truly just fighting on foreign land and not the destruction of home.

This is the image I am searching for. This is what went up in smoke less than a year before my father's death. These are the details I have kept hidden from my writing, trying hard to stay with the vertical. But life is not always perpendicular to the horizon. And life in war especially not. At some point the story I am beginning to remember must be laid out in words across the page.

"Do you remember anything from Daddy's visit that June?" I ask Janice on the phone. She tells me the two of them drove to Cincinnati together after my father's visit in order to see his old friend Bob Salzer — or was it Bob Salzman? I ask her — who used to live across the hall from us in Germany. He owned a bar in Cincinnati, and Janice and my father stayed in an apartment above the bar. She remembers the jukebox with all the 45 RPM records and how she loved listening to the music of the Four Tops. It is what she remembers the most, she says. After Cincinnati they went to Washington, D.C., where she thinks he stayed for a while, and she flew on to New Jersey to spend the summer with Aunt Val and Uncle Bob.

"Did we see him again before he left for Vietnam that December?" I ask. She says that it must have been during basketball season when he came to visit again because she remembers he went to a game with us at the high school. He wore his short-sleeved khaki uniform and was cold in the Illinois winter.

Then she says, "He wanted us to go to Germany with him." For a few seconds I can't talk. Had I known this before and buried it like so many other details? Why is it I am unable to recall what my sister so vividly remembers?

She continues telling me their conversation: "If you go, your sisters will come, he said. Come with me to Germany. I can have my orders changed to go there instead of Vietnam." Janice told him that our mother needed us. "But I need you too," he said. When she told him our mother needed us more, he pleaded. He said we could fly back from Germany and spend the summers with her. In the end, Janice told him no, and he never mentioned it again. "Now when I look back I think he desperately wanted to know we loved him. That he still had a family," Janice says. "But it was a horrible decision for a fourteen-year-old girl to make."

I begin to remember some things about that last visit as I speak with Janice. My fragmented consciousness falls into narrative. He wore black Vietnamese pajamas and a Buddha necklace around his neck. He ate rice while sitting on the floor. I introduced him to my boyfriend, Steve, and thought it strange when my father, this man in an exotic costume, gave us a curfew for the school dance. Steve shook his hand at our apartment door while my father eyed him up and down. When I came in late, my father lectured me – not with anger but with concern in his voice – about the dangers out there for young girls. I wasn't accustomed to such immediate concern, such fatherly advice, and I wasn't sure I liked it.

I think we talked a little while at that midnight hour, but I can't be sure of the things we said. I wish I had told him about the night a stranger chased me on a dark street. Even though I made it to my grandmother's house before anything happened, I wish I had told him just how frightened I had been, how I had wanted him there to protect me. I could have told him as well about the time a stranger fondled me while I tried to swim in the Atlantic Ocean and I couldn't get away. Maybe my father could have told me how to defend myself.

Days after Janice's phone call, I remember a glimmer of recognition of my father's loneliness as he and I talked that night after the dance. I see him lying prone on the couch with a book on his chest, wearing his reading glasses as I stood by the steps. The carved coffee table he had once bought for our apartment in Germany stood in front of him. It was a scene that could have been taken out of our past together, only now it all seemed worlds away from either of us. For a very quick unspoken moment I felt both of our losses. I knew in that fleeting second that my father had his books and the army, but he didn't have us anymore – and we didn't have him. At the same time I was envious of his solitary life, wishing I could walk away like he was going to, from this dirty apartment with its empty refrigerator and stacks of unironed laundry. I wanted in that quick second of insight to go with him. His visit had brought a sudden outburst of hunger for him, and I was aware of it as fast as I buried the desire.

I have no recollection of his leaving town. It was more like a wind that blew in and then blew out. More like a spirit that I'm not sure was there at all. Very soon afterward in December 1966, my father went back to Vietnam for the last time. His few photographs of that tour of duty aren't labeled like the ones from the years before, and I can't be sure they are even of his last months there. I notice numbers on the back of the pictures as if they are code for something. I wonder now as I look at them if I am imagining it or do I actually see sadness in my father's eyes? Do I see a look of seriousness, as if he is saying this is a grave business and I'm not sure now exactly why I am here?

Janice sends me copies of letters she's saved from those early months in 1967 written before our father's death. He mentions the upcoming Tet – the lunar New Year celebrated by the Vietnamese and Chinese – in his January letter. Just paragraphs away, he asks if we have received the encyclopedias he ordered for us. In February's letter he tells us that he sent our mother some papers to sign and have notarized so we could be released from all liability on our house in Fayetteville. He was planning to take his company back to the delta on a short operation and remembered that the last time he was there he was only twenty-five meters from a VC battalion. Then he switches to his hopes about getting to the post exchange so he can buy a tape recorder and hear our voices.

It is his letter written exactly two weeks before his death that I search through over and over again, looking for some clue I must have missed. He encloses money for us — five dollars for each girl and one dollar for Wesley — and mentions that his unit is short of men. He writes that he has blood poisoning in his right arm and just had a couple of teeth extracted, which "was very painful because a bone fragment was working loose." Sergeant Laudacina, he says, had called him from Saigon. He brings the short letter to a sudden halt because of a formation but mentions for the second time in that letter that he hopes to hear from us soon.

I want suddenly to go back in time and know why it is I must save every word that comes to us from across the ocean. I want to know then why it is I must tell him to come home, that maybe we can all start again and go back to Flint Kaserne, where life was once good to our family. That he must label his photographs so I will know just what his last months were like. I want to go back and reach my small arms across oceans and continents to touch my father one more time before the end. I want, like a prisoner before the execution, to speak to him one more time. A scream sits below the surface of my throat as I write this, wishing it could be heard down through the years.

I filter through time and try hard to think back to those months of January, February, and early March 1967 before my father was killed. I recall a vague uneasiness, a building discomfort I felt for life. I remember walking down the halls of Harrisburg High School in a fog, wondering just who was this person who was now flunking Latin and could barely care about geometry. It was as if I was running toward death without knowing it, as if memories of my father were sliding off my skin, as if I could already hear the explosions in the distance.

I remember not being able to get out of bed some mornings because I was so tired I could barely move. The doctor diagnosed anemia, and surely it was, but there was more to it than that. My body began to attack itself rather than the world, and months after my father's death several doctors were to ask me if there had been a recent tragedy, one that might have eaten away at my gums at such an early age or thrown my body into constant hypoglycemic shock. The world was disordered, I want now to tell those doctors. I want them to know that what they saw inside me, that small disordered immune system, was really a picture of the world I'd come to see. What I reflected inside my body was what I couldn't begin to say yet.

Another scene begs to be set down. It is during our days in D.C. when we came in 1969 for my father's posthumously awarded Medal of Honor. Another family, as well, had come for their son/brother's, given on the same day. We toured the White House together, walking side by side through the rooms. I remember we barely spoke; there seemed so little to say. They appeared awkward in their dress clothes, so solemn and quiet. I could barely speak to my sisters at that point about the war and what all this meant, so I couldn't begin to speak to this family from Alabama I didn't know. In the photographs taken that day by the military, I see this intermingling of strangers standing together but alone in the same room as the White House guide points at what he wants us to see.

In a Polynesian restaurant that evening, our military escort, who was seemingly so friendly and helpful, spoke to Janice and me at the end of our long table about the oldest daughter of the other family — how she had had an illegitimate child. He implied in his voice, or at least I thought so then, that she was white trash, that no wonder she felt uncomfortable and out of place here in the nation's capital. It was clearly a belittling, a shadow intruded upon the medal. I wondered in that moment just what it was that this all-knowing institution knew about me. What was it that Big Brother knew but wasn't saying? I understood right then and there that he was trying to take away something from this hero and this hero's family. By his condescending remarks, our handsome escort was denying this family from Alabama their suffering and interfering with their honor.

He spoke to Janice and me as if we were different, as if our well-dressed family led by my articulate, handsome uncle was somehow pure and therefore more deserving. But we knew differently. We were not only medal bearers, but we had our secrets and our civilian sufferings as well. This shameful sense of secrets was to be a future obstacle for me in my writing about that medal, about my mother, about my father. I was terrified of casting any shadow on my father's Medal of Honor and worried that it would be taken away from him. I had to protect him with my silence. Eventually I felt as if I had no freedom to use the information I had. Homer mostly left out civilian suffering in his poem about war, Finvola tells me on the phone as I describe this scene to her. I was doing the same, drawing a line down the middle with my father's army life on one side and our civilian life on the other, as if one touching the other would wash it all away and my father would be left with nothing.

Between then and now I have found what Finvola calls my "narrative rights." I have brought together my shattered knowledge and discovered I have the strength to look at my father's photographs without being destroyed, that speaking about them is my way of finding all of our lives from that time. I have mixed the colors from both parts of my life — the military and the civilian — and have walked through the muted but true color it makes. I have run back to let the past catch up with me before it is too late. I have met Kuan Kung, the ancient Chinese god of both war and literature. I have felt his two great winds of yin and yang.

Along that road of discovery I have found my father. I have reclaimed something not yet buried. I have, as my father so often did with his translations of foreign languages, found intelligence through writing. It is this connection that leads me through my father's photographs, weaving in and out of his life until we are face to face, as if I could reach through thin air and touch him again. His spirit, sometimes dressed in Oriental garb and sometimes in uniform but always with his Buddha necklace and dog tags, blows back into my life. We stand in the light of my writing and I embrace his pain as well as my own. Within that embrace we are rejoined, and there is release for both of us.

Sacrifice

It's not as though I haven't pictured my father's death many times. But when I see a National Archives official sketch of the scene of action, it doesn't register. I slip the forms back into the envelope. Two days later I bring out the papers again and stare at the map like I'm looking at a fourth grade textbook and can't figure out the legend. Interprovincial Route #13 is to the north, the Song Be River is to the west. From the river to the ambush site is approximately three kilometers. Small boxes mark two abandoned vehicles along the trail, and there are large Xs to represent Captain Canale, Sergeant Hallberg, and the two Vietnamese interpreters. As if this were a pirate's treasure map, someone formed tiny dashes into a circle and wrote the word "tree" with an arrow. There is an X for my father before the action and an X for the "VC before the action." Then I notice a single X used to represent both "VC and SFC Hosking after action." A picture is worth a thousand words, as the saying goes. Still, it doesn't register.

I read the notes Major Harribey wrote up for a motivational analysis to accompany a recommendation for a Medal of Honor. I read each typed word fast at first and then slowly. There is a tension between my silence and the necessary disclosure. My writing room grows even more quiet except for some water draining through the upstairs pipes. I picture these men I never met, accompanying my father's body to the Ninety-third Evacuation Hospital to make a positive identification of the remains inside the black body bag. I picture Harribey interviewing Captain Canale while he drives a jeep at the same time. It is 1400 hours on March 21, 1967, and if my civilian mind hasn't forgotten, that means it is two o'clock in the afternoon.

Major Harribey writes that although Canale had been slightly wounded in the groin by the blast action of the grenade, he is completely alert and able to answer questions. Canale stresses over and over again that he was certain that SFC Hosking had known full well the danger he risked when he grabbed the VC. He believed he did it anyway because it had to be done. Harribey delivers him to the Third Surgical Hospital at Bien Hoa and then finds Staff Sergeant Hallberg to ask him the same questions. Hallberg volunteers that Hosking had reacted instantaneously and that he was convinced Hosking had been well aware of the danger involved. He said he knew that Hosking had a habit of making rapid decisions when needed and acting upon them without hesitation. The only thing Hallberg and Canale could not agree on was how far off exactly the abandoned vehicles were, and whether the interpreters were right behind Hallberg or if they were some five meters away.

The recommendation for a Medal of Honor was finalized and signed by Lieutenant Colonel Huddleston and forwarded to headquarters in Saigon. On April 5, a request for clarification of some points was requested. Again Captain Canale was interviewed. By this time, Sergeant Hallberg was missing in action. Canale stated that in knowing Hosking both in garrison and on combat operations, he saw that he could evaluate a situation, make a decision, and execute it quickly, and that he was obviously an experienced combat infantryman. He stated that Hosking could easily have taken no positive action, just yelled "grenade" and fallen to the ground behind the tree, where he would have been "relatively" safe from the blast.

When Harribey went to interview the two Vietnamese interpreters, he found that Mr. San had quit toward the end of March and simply left no forwarding address. Mr. Dao Quoc Hoa, born in Saigon on April 20, 1941, had requested and received a transfer to another A detachment. He told Harribey he had done that because there had been continuous combat operations and heavy casualties in the Mike Force companies.

Mr. Hoa said that the prisoner had told them that he was merely on the trail to take some tools and parts off the abandoned vehicles. Hosking knew the prisoner was lying because he had already checked the truck and there were no tools left on it. Also, as the prisoner had no tools with him, he could not have expected to take any parts off it. Mr. Hoa remembers that someone at that point mentioned to Hosking that this was the same man who had been apprehended some months before during a rifle fire at the camp east of the ambush site. He had been turned over to the local district chief then. Mr. Hoa verified that Hosking had untied the prisoner to prepare to take him back to Cau Song Be. The prisoner grabbed a grenade from Hosking's suspenders, pulled the pin, and started toward Captain Canale and the others. Hosking grabbed the prisoner around the chest and threw him to the ground before he covered the prisoner's body with his own, Mr. Hoa said. The grenade went off just as Hosking landed on top of the prisoner.

Major Harribey asked Mr. Hoa if Hosking could have saved himself by any other action. He could have thrown himself backward and not been hurt or only hurt slightly when the grenade went off, Mr. Hoa answered. Had Hosking yelled anything when the prisoner grabbed the grenade? No, Mr. Hoa answered. He said that he was within a few meters of the entire incident and saw everything that took place.

After interviewing some other men who had known my father for many years, Harribey concluded that my father's act that March 21, 1967, was consistent with his past performance of duty. It was exactly what everyone expected my father would do under such circumstances. Before Harribey signed his name to the official report, he wrote: "He could have alerted the others in the group who were all aware of the VC's actions as they were watching him, by shouting 'grenade' and without cowardice taking cover to his rear behind a tree, but he unselfishly and without hesitation took the proper actions to save his comrade's lives."

There it is. What I have been searching for all along. The truth within Harribey's sentence. My father's actions were not bravado, were not suicide, were not family induced, were not fatalism, were not their own form of cowardice. What my father carried around with him was a knowledge of how to proceed in such matters. His notion of normal gave him no choice in what he did. While the others observed, it fell to him. Saving his own skin was not an option. In a split second, this warrior, this man of *mētis*, assessed the situation and performed a timely intervention. His action was embedded in the ancient Greek symbolic order. My father was that X.

A month following my father's posthumously awarded Medal of Honor, my aunt and uncle received a letter from Charlene Canale, Captain Canale's wife. It was a short, hand-written letter that came from the heart of this intermediary between soldier and family-of-fallen-soldier. She mentioned that the Medal of Honor was a small reward for a life, but that it could be a constant reminder of the kind of soldier and man she had heard my father was. Before ending the letter with her prayers for us, she wrote that it was difficult for a man to live with a debt he knew he could never repay.

I know now without a doubt that my father's life dealt with the ancient model of sacrifice. Like the tales of old, he called it by its real name. He never excused himself from its terror. Nor did he expect life to be anything else.

Had I read this formal action report before I wrote this book, it would have been just another piece of paper. But as I have searched my father's photographs, searched through his life, searched through my own soul, I know now what it was my father did and why he did it. I am the writer/daughter who can decipher this report now. As Snake's daughter I am not the same person I was when I began this journey. My consciousness is no longer divided. There is a feeling within me of having come home, a feeling of having found something very precious and irreplaceable that I once lost.

Dream

n my vivid dream I see a harmless-looking snake slithering around on the floor of my childhood apartment in Germany. I am not afraid to pick it up, so I do and then hang it on my door. It suddenly looks like a twisted walking stick. The doorbell rings, and a group of friendly people greet me at the bottom of the steps. I kiss everyone. Then I notice my father standing in the back of the group. He is quiet and looks into my eyes. He is not in uniform and doesn't carry any weapon. I run up to him and kiss him gently on the cheek. We embrace, and I feel a reuniting that joins our severed lives.

In the morning I call Finvola and tell her about this dream. She reminds me of the caduceus — the staff with twined snakes, the symbol of healing, the walking stick carried by Mercury, who was the messenger of the gods. I know as we speak that I am Snake's daughter. I have written my father home.

An Attempted Ending

he man who went down an Olympic ski jump in Germany in a box is the same man who counted the clothing that went in the backpacks of the soldiers he trained in Vietnam. The man who once hit my mother in the nose was the same man who danced with her tenderly. I was awake down the hall as they yelled into the night he hit her. Later, he said he would rather have been shot than to have done that to the woman he adored. Such are the complexities of love.

The man who sometimes drank himself into oblivion was the same man who remembered all the details of a jungle operation. The man who would jump to attention whenever an officer came into the room was the same man who got the highest grade in a University of Maryland military science class in which he was the only enlisted man to participate. This same man who had opportunities to become an officer chose to stay "at the bottom with the best." He was also the man who said he wanted to be with his family very much but went to Vietnam three times knowing the statistics of death.

This same man once bought gold cuff links for a Mexican / American soldier who had saved his life. "Your Dad loved that guy," Michael O'Connor, who had been on the same team with my father in Germany, wrote me. "You have to understand that guys didn't buy each other gifts back then." My father is this same man whose great-uncle Albert had left his son Wesley with his brother in New Jersey while he drifted across the country. History, something my father was fond of reading, would repeat itself when my father left his son, Wesley, with his brother in New Jersey.

It's not that I understand all that my father did or why he lived the way he did; and it's not that writing this book answered all that for me. Just as the aperture of a lens limits the amount of light that can enter the camera and the lens itself circumscribes what you can see, there is a limit to how I can know my father. I never let on as I wrote about him, not even to myself, that what I wanted was to come up with a sketch of simple answers. I wanted from my writing about my father's life answers to all life's labyrinthine questions — his and mine. I wanted answers that placed the yes's on one side and the no's on another; but if anything, all the telephone calls from strangers who knew my father, all the books I read about war, all the correspondence I had with Finvola, and all the photographs I studied led me farther away from that kind of simplicity.

I know my father less now in the ways I thought I knew him — the hero, that Special Forces guy called Snake who was awarded the Medal of Honor. Except for my collection of childhood images all neatly filed in my mind like my father's photograph collection, I knew my father for a long time through that medal, and yet I rarely spoke about it — the object itself, or what it represents. "How is it you never told me he was awarded the Medal of Honor after all we've talked about your father's life?" Finvola asked me in astonishment one day sitting on my front porch. I tried to tell her the uncomplicated truth, which reveals mine and my country's shame around a war many agree we had no business to fight. It had become a habit not to say the Medal of Honor out loud. Talking about the medal involved finding language that hadn't been created yet. "Finding that there are no words for something you have to say is to feel the full weight of the negative coming down on you," she was to write me later.

Finally, to discuss the medal was to discuss blood — that real blood that comes with any medal, no matter what war, in what time, in what country. It was to remember why he was awarded the medal and to add a blown-apart body to my mind's store of images. Even trained soldiers choose to forget such things.

To not talk about the medal was to lock myself away in safety under glass, as the real medal is protected now on my uncle's living room wall. It was to keep life neatly divided because I couldn't bear the dark walk in between.

I didn't want to speak of the medal because I feared another kind of giving my father away, piece by piece, until he was completely gone, and no one would feel then that they needed to know anything else about him. I've been afraid that people who never met my father will think they knew him: another bloody Hollywood image of a tiger-stripe uniformed Special Forces soldier, an image that supposedly tells the whole story. They will forget my father as I feared doing myself, so that I wouldn't even be able to pass his memory on to my children or to my country. So instead, I kept the medal a secret as if in doing so I was keeping my father safe from harm, not mentioning it and barely able, until recently, to cough out the words Vietnam War.

"When Gail works out that medal, she'll work out the whole war," a woman in my writing group once said casually, sitting on the floor of her living room where we were meeting to discuss our essays. When she said that my eyes suddenly met hers and locked for a few seconds, the way you sometimes do when you've shared a truth with someone. What she said has haunted me ever since like a puzzle demanding a solution.

While my father's journey was one underwritten by the flesh, mine has been one of the spirit. He risked his body constantly from his first step into Fort Shelby, Mississippi, to his last steps in the jungles of Vietnam. All those endless push-ups, the jumps out of airplanes, the long marches with heavy backpacks, the climbs up jagged mountains, the walks through the pitch-black nights not ever knowing when he might trip a claymore mine. Muscle by muscle, he gave the military what it asked of him from the beginning: his strength, his muscle-trained courage, his life.

My own risks have been different. I walked away from a teaching job in pursuit of something undefined, something beating insistently against the walls of my skin. I risked speaking with strangers who would open a path between the subject of war and my life. I risked really looking at my father's photographs and having that act of seeing call me into action. As Richard Powers wrote in his novel of World War I, *Three Farmers on Their Way to a Dance*, my search through my father's photographs made me risk a "synchroneity with the photographer the way a museum-case glass, slicing through a beehive, invites us to live in the colony." Finally, I risked extending his story into mine.

Finvola wrote me after I wrote her about the explosive, murderous rage I sometimes carry within me: "the daughter/writer asks about the source of her rage and likens the feeling it brings to a combat situation, such as the one which killed the hero/father. The hero is not only an illustrious warrior, but the central actor in an event. The rage of the daughter/writer, an explosive murderous rage, is the desire to become the hero, the central actor in the event of her own life, to end the motion between that rage and the long night's reconnaissance during which the rage builds to the breaking point again." She writes me that this daughter/writer is battling to become the writer/daughter. I know as I read it that she is right — that only in that exchange will the displacement occur so that my sufferings, as she says, "can be taken up in the economy of the writer, and the daughter can occupy the space where heroism and abandonment live daily side by side: in writing."

Most of my life I've not been the one who skis down just-a-little-steeper hill each time like my father insisted on doing himself. I choose rather to stay at a plateau, satisfied with my mediocre physical ability. I'm the one who likes things neat, doesn't go for that extra beer at midnight, and makes sure the laundry is caught up. I surrender myself to the expected form I think I'm supposed to have, the way my father had to do in the army, but I deeply desire rebellion at the same time, the way he did within the army structure itself. This paradox churns me up and often makes me uncomfortable in either direction. I think my friends might not know this about me, but they've not seen how taut the strings of my heart are, how afraid I am of spontaneous change, as if it could be spontaneous combustion and destroy me the way I imagine it did my father.

I think I've been in mourning since the day I heard from that young soldier's lips that my father had been killed in action near the Song Be River. If grief at that stage is mostly wordless, that's where I was all these years until the search through my father's images sparked my own words and set them free. The lens I've used to look out of in that grief has been narrow. It's kept those who fought and those who didn't fight on separate sides of my mind. It saw the Vietnam War as something apart from the collective history of our country.

Opening up that narrow lens, like the world I traveled through with my father's photographs, introduced me to that larger circle. It brought into view all the names on the wall in D.C., and all the soldiers and nurses who came to Vietnam and left behind pieces of their lives. This new light allowed me to enter the circle of my civilian colleagues who were seemingly untouched by the war. It gave me the courage to step in and announce my life, my background, that medal.

Finvola writes me about the medal and the war: "You were presented with an almost irreconcilable difficulty, one which the entire society in which we live has not solved. Why do you think the ancient Greeks were at such pains to sort all this out?"

What I've needed to do all along was to let that medal out of the glass, to touch its ribbons, and to study its design. I've needed to let it be what it is, what it always was: one man's attempt to make right in the world when surrounded by insanity, one man's love for the men he entrusted with his life. The medal speaks of his desire to make right with a part of his life where he couldn't with the rest of it. In the end, he did what he sent me to Sunday school every week of my childhood to learn: that there is love greater than we know or think we know. And it is that love which allows one human being to give his life for another — not in any perfect way, but bringing to that love all the imperfections any of us ever have.

I believe a heartache will always rise from the recesses of my memory every March 21, the day my father was killed. The ache will return. Nothing about the date or the clothes I will choose to wear on that day will tell the world of my father's memory. Nothing about my face will speak of jungle villages he saw. Only the equinox will come and with it the crack between time and memory and dogwood trees that my father never had a chance to plant on the empty lot he left behind for duty. There will be no guns saluting in the background, no ambush to provide a way out. I will walk through all the March twenty-firsts of the future and melt into the long winding roads I can't see yet.

I am destined to remember my father in his prime, forever a soldier. With his early death, I don't have to think of nursing homes or cancer wards. But what I've missed is telling him about the surprises I find in the places he never saw — like that time sitting below the Parthenon as a newlywed and listening to the Vienna Philharmonic by moonlight, or the time I saw the White Cloud Mountains in Idaho and they took my breath away.

The births of my children brought the strangest sense of connection for me. I felt at times as if my children came out of nowhere and belonged nowhere. I fluctuated between knowing it was my responsibility to pass on every detail of my parents' lives and pretending that it didn't matter anyway. But then at some point, I caught sight of a spider's silk thread in the sunlight and I wanted to weave it from my parents to my children. The writing gave a place for the silk threads to attach themselves.

I look at the death notices of my great-great-grandparents that lie in a file Janice gave me. Lists of names of offspring, names I might choose again if only I had time for one hundred children of my own, stand out in succession. There are those who died at birth, those who died along the way, and those who went on to produce their own children. I see the reasons for their deaths:

carcinoma of the jaw, eclampsia, heart failure. There are dates and countries of marriage. So far from that time, I find it interesting, but not so the death notices of my parents. Those I do not own — I have memorized them the way I want to memorize their lives.

I am not the first in my family to need the connecting lines between the past and the present. In my search to find my father, I see that there have been others who saved family tree information. There has always been someone who came before me and cherished the family connection. It's as if someone put the facts aside for me, waiting for my pen to be ready.

Like my father's photographs, the family tree challenges me to know all the tenses at the same time: the past, the present, and the future. I come to know from both the pictures and the documents what Susan Sontag once wrote: that "once-alive body radiated light which reaches through, touching us like the delayed rays of a star." I present that now to my children.

What they will find when they are ready to see is not a formal biography of my father, not my full-fledged autobiography, but elements of both. When I began this project, I was naive enough to think that pure observation and description of my father's photographs could tell the whole story, and I wouldn't have to dig any deeper. What I found out was that his story and my story kept crossing paths. I was continually brought back to myself as if I had to ask, What does this mean about *my* life? What can *I* make of this?

I was thirteen years old when my father first left for Vietnam. The war took over both of our lives from that moment, and we were not ever to live together as father and daughter again for more than a few months at a time. It would take me twenty-six years to begin the search back to him — to find my father beyond the hero and beyond the man everyone spoke of as "an excellent soldier." It would take me all that time to articulate a collected and collective shame and a silence I could no longer bear. Finally, it would take me that long to feel both the stirrings of a warrior and his daughter not yet at peace. Feeling his presence as I write was and remains an experience one might label as spiritual or otherworldly, nothing I can put my finger on. Perhaps in that way, it is true that our parents are concerned with us even in their death.

My father wasn't a political man; he rarely spoke about the government itself. Yet he was involved in the politics of this country every day of his military life. What he despised was hypocrisy among the leaders, "buttering up the higher-ups," and the manipulative ways some soldiers worked for job advancement. His was a smaller world based on his friends and the principles he would not let go of. It rarely got him a raise or another stripe. It was often his own failures that took those earned stripes away. His life pulled constantly in directions of paradox and tension.

My life is not one of politics either, except if you believe like the writer Natalie Goldberg that writing is in itself a political act. It cuts through our illusions and calls things the way they are. This paying attention to detail, "caressing the divine details," as Nabokov wrote, gets us into the muddy, real lives of those we've loved.

Had my father lived through the Vietnam War, perhaps he would have spent the rest of his life struggling to express what he saw and felt. Perhaps it is my writing that sets into motion a vast wave of his desire to be understood. In doing so, I have become the writer I was meant to be. As my friend wrote me, "It's as if your father's life made you a daughter, and his death made you a writer." I am trying to restore both our shattered selves.

I finish writing this late at night in a third-floor room of my Victorian house on a quiet street in upstate New York. A summer's night breeze blows through the window next to me. I lean into the back of a small navy blue love seat and look at a Chinese print on rice paper that a friend once bought at the Great Wall of China. A white basket of artificial red, white, and blue flowers sits on top of a nearby bookshelf. The basket with "Medal of Honor" written in gold letters on a red ribbon had been delivered to me on the opening night of my photo/essay exhibit, *Snake's Daughter: The Roads in and out of War*. A small note from my father's friend Mike McCarthy is still attached: "In memory of The Snake."

As this night gets closer to the midnight hour and I move with the clock into the early morning hours, I still wonder how to get this book right. I feel as if I still don't know or can never know all the details of my father's life, nor have I solved it all so that I can finish. Its incompleteness swirls me back to the beginning, always with the hope I can stop death, always with the fantasy that my father is nearby as long as the manuscript pages sit on my desk. Shadows of his past continue to cross my path with letters from his soldier friends, with the faces of my two sons, with the similar ways I sometimes catch myself behaving. I come to my father's life tonight with the openness of a writer, the humility of middle age, and the desires of a daughter. I see both our flawed characters as I move slowly off the stage of perfection where I had once placed myself.

On the wall above the guest bed in this same room is a framed drawing I once did when I took the drawing class I've written about. It's a drawing of rose hips still attached to prickly-stemmed branches. Some of the leaves are fully green and drawn with great detail. Others are in pencil as if they're fading even as I look at them — or is it that they are coming to life silently as I don't watch? Some of the drawing is done on the paper and some is done on the ripped collage of paper laid on top. It's like looking down through the layers of life — like I'm peeking through the spaces and strata of my own heart.

The computer on the nearby desk holds my words and prints them out in ways that would have been totally unavailable in my father's time. Inside that same computer are games my sons play — war games where guns rarely miss targets and heroes take adventurous journeys my sons like to follow. They live with the illusion of eternity — death blotted out from their young minds as if a large paper towel soaked the thought up. They draw a curtain, an impossible-to-destroy curtain, and they dream of shooting at make-believe targets forever. Age and war packed up my illusions and dropped them out to sea. My father learned about the trail of death from the beginning of his soldiering. It has been said that the young who fight a war are never young again, and in that way my father was never young in the time I knew him.

My sons give me a perfunctory nod, a half-listen, when I tell them stories of my life. It is the ache not necessarily of pain but beauty as well that I want them to know about. I want them to hear the stories I carry within me, the people, the tears at three in the morning. I want them to see mountain tops they've not seen yet and glimpses of history even as it's happening. I want them to know my father.

The cat cries outside the door and wants in. Doesn't she know I need quiet at this hour? Not just quiet, but I need to feel as if the whole world has disappeared and it's only me and the pen left. Otherwise the words stay inside, as defended as they used to be. All I hear is the sound of their beating from the inside out again. I fiddle with the Buddha necklace my father gave me so long ago and which now hangs around my neck on a gold chain. After all its time sitting in a green velvet box inside my top dresser drawer, I've recaptured it and brought it back into my life.

How have I been able to speak of war here in a place of such tranquillity? What have I been able to say to my generation, who hated the war and sometimes failed to see the difference between the war and the warriors? Never have I felt so lonely than in the aftermath of Vietnam.

It was a very long war. Not because I ever saw combat, but because the telling of this war got buried just as the pain reached my heart. It has taken me years to find words, inadequate as they feel, to express something about the man I knew as my father. Mostly it's taken me that long to realize how desperate I've been to hold up my father's picture, demanding that others look. He wasn't a killer in the Hollywood shoot-'em-up kind of way, and he didn't love war. He went because for him his world came down to the men on his right and the men on his left, and for them he was willing to give his own life. He lived in a world where Ares, the Greek god of war, kills those who kill, and in a world where each man counts more than anything else to those around him. In finding words about my father and in holding up his photograph, I am uncovering the others who counted to many.

I grew up in that closed, small world of the military where soldiers are never forgotten. But I cannot return to the fortress now. I must come back from my childhood and remember my father from the place I am now. It is in the writing life of my adulthood that I can recognize my father's loyalty, his courage, the way he bit his nails and laughed in a deep-voice kind of way. The way he sent scores of letters home from the battlefield, always ending with: "I love and miss you, love, Daddy."

All my silent years later, finally, and with abiding sorrow, I salute him.

To My Father

remember sitting across from you at the table while you polished the brass on your uniform. I had a pencil in my hand as
I did my homework. Once in awhile I'd look up from the page
and watch you. We didn't speak. You wore your Second World
War undershirt tucked into what you called your "knock around
fatigues." In spite of the tiny holes around the neck's edge, you
couldn't get rid of those army clothes that defined to all of us who
you were. I was aware of how intent you were on the task before
you. It was evening, and there was the ease of being together, the
comfort of our routines, and the preparations for the next day.

Again I remember the two of us together. I was older and had
come home from a date and found you stretched out and reading
on our couch. You were a visitor — we both knew you'd be leaving
any day again for Vietnam. You wore your black Vietnamese pajamas, and a book lay across your chest. Except for the outfit, I had
seen you in that position many times. But this time the essence of
some Buddhist spirit rose from you as you lowered your reading
glasses and gazed over at me. We didn't speak about anything
in particular. I remember the air of leave-taking in the room,
the solace that you were there, and a sorrow about where history
found us.

What you might have said to a son that night about the war, I
do not know. As a daughter I wasn't to go to war. It rested with
you. What comes forward to me is the domestic: the Vietnamese
costume, the Buddha necklace, the homework at the dining room
table, the attention to details, the book laid across your chest.
Now that I come to the end of this writing, I struggle with the
leave-taking. I am not accustomed to leaving you. You were the
one who always left. Now it is I who must be intent on the task before me.

I once viewed the war from as far away as I could be, locked up
within myself like a prisoner. Finding my way to your photographs and my willingness to study them has freed my buried
words. I have moved from the distance to the close-up. I have
rekindled what Homer called "the slow fires of longing." I am no
longer quiet and passive. That has always been the risk. It was, I

New Jersey Vietnam War Memorial.

see, the risks you took as well. Those hazards brought your ultimate death. As I finish this writing, I struggle to understand how I take the risk of ending. Does it mean that to finish is to die?

How do I resolve a soldier father's life in a villainous war? What is the resolution after this long journey? What is it I have found at the end? Your actions transcended the war. Your human heroic act stood alone. It was basic, full of risk, and full of love. I see now that I must transcend the war by living. I must rise above it by writing beyond this book. That is the risk I take in coming to the end. I must continue to live up close to the details of life and not to close them off again. I am the resolution. I conquer your death through my own personal acts. I am more than a daughter of a dead soldier, just like you were more than a soldier in a hideous war.

Only now does this journey come to an end. I have completed the action. This book was not meant as a confession, a mere telling of our family tales. Writing this book was meant as an action to your death, and an action for my life. You were the one who taught me early on to complete the operation. You instilled in me the desire to find my way to the end from the beginning. Now I have prepared your body properly for burial. What was once blown apart by war has been made whole again. And so it is I finish writing what has absorbed me now for many years.

Love,
Gail

BIBLIOGRAPHY

Barthes, Roland. *Camera Lucida*. New York: Noonday Press, 1981.

Bows, Ray A. *Vietnam: Military Lore 1959–1973*. Hanover, Mass.: Bows and Sons Publishing, 1988.

Detiennb, Marcel, and Jean-Pierre Vernat. *Cunning Intelligence in Greek Culture and Society*. Trans. Janet Lloyd. Chicago: University of Chicago Press, 1991.

Eisenhower, Dwight D. *The Crusade in Europe*. Garden City, N.Y.: Doubleday, 1948.

Fall, Bernard B. *Hell in a Very Small Place: The Siege of Dien Bien Phu*. Philadelphia: Lippincott, 1967.

Gray, J. Glenn. *The Warriors: Reflections on Men in Battle*. New York: Harper and Row, 1959.

Hanley, Lynne. *Writing War: Fiction, Gender and Memory*. Amherst: University of Massachusetts Press, 1991.

Herr, Michael. *Dispatches*. 1st ed. New York: Knopf, 1977.

Homer. *The Iliad*. Trans. Robert Fitzgerald. Garden City, N.Y.: Doubleday, 1974.

Lesy, Michael. *Rescues: The Lives of Heroes*. New York: Farrar, Straus and Giroux, 1991.

Nicolai, Georg Friedrich. *The Biology of War*. New York: Century Co., 1918.

Ninh, Bao. *The Sorrow of War: A Novel of North Vietnam*. Trans. Phan Thanh Hao. 1st American ed. New York: Pantheon Books, 1995.

O'Brien, Tim. *Going after Cacciato*. New York: Delacorte Press, 1978.

Powers, Richard. *Three Farmers on Their Way to a Dance*. New York: Beech Tree Books, 1985.

Shay, Jonathan. *Achilles in Vietnam: Combat Trauma and the Undoing of Character*. New York: Scribner, 1994.

Sontag, Susan. *On Photography*. New York: Farrar, Straus and Giroux, 1977.

Time-Life. *This Fabulous Century: 1960–1970*. Vol. 7. New York: Time-Life Books, 1970.

Weil, Simone. *The Iliad, or the Poem of Force*. Pendle Hill pamphlet 91, Wallingford, Penn.

Wertsch, Mary Edwards. *Military Brats: Legacies of Childhood inside the Fortress*. New York: Harmony Books, 1991.

SINGULAR LIVES

The Anti-Warrior: A Memoir *By Milt Felsen*

Black Eagle Child: The Facepaint Narratives
By Ray A. Young Bear

China Dreams: Growing Up Jewish in Tientsin
By Isabelle Maynard

Fly in the Buttermilk: The Life Story of Cecil Reed
By Cecil A. Reed with Priscilla Donovan

In My Father's Study *By Ben Orlove*

In Search of Susanna *By Suzanne L. Bunkers*

Journey into Personhood *By Ruth Cameron Webb*

Letters from Togo *By Susan Blake*

A Lucky American Childhood *By Paul Engle*

A Prairie Populist: The Memoirs of Luna Kellie
Edited by Jane Taylor Nelsen

Snake's Daughter: The Roads in and out of War
By Gail Hosking Gilberg

Taking Part: A Twentieth-Century Life *By Robert Josephy*

Tales of an American Hobo *By Charles Elmer Fox*

Unfriendly Fire *By Peg Mullen*

The Warsaw Sparks *By Gary Gildner*